A MUSLIM ON THE BRIDGE

ON BEING AN IRAQI-ARAB MUSLIM IN THE TWENTY-FIRST CENTURY

Praise for *A Muslim on the Bridge*:

With almost a quarter of the world's population embracing Islam, Ali Shakir's work provides a timely insight into the dilemmas facing contemporary Muslims caught between the desire for modernity and respect for tradition. Having set out to determine whether other religions might be "better, worse, or just like Islam," his journey is also an articulate exploration of the rivalry between monotheistic faiths that has always existed and, along with politics, kept the flames of hatred in the Middle East burning for so long. He particularly examines the Koran, whose teachings are wide open to interpretation, being written in a language that is different from the ordinary Arabic of today, and focuses on the "most-quoted verse on Muslim bigotry world-wide," which states that they should avoid dealings and friendships with non-believers in every possible way. The Prophet Mohammed acknowledged both Judaism and Christianity on several occasions, he says; the command-ment said nothing about friendships, being merely an instruction not to take non-believers as protectors or leaders. It is hard to disagree with his conclusion that between Muslims, Jews, and Christians it is extremely difficult to determine who are the promised descen-dants of Abraham. This book is a well-written collection of sensitive musings weaving personal experiences in a diary/narrative form. He touches on subjects as great as the meaning of Arabic culture in general, the Arab Spring, and what that has brought to those who sought a more secular way of life. Tackling the question of men's rights over women, illicit love, feminism, polygamy, homosexuality, as well as the wearing of the *abaya*, he also finds room for the dying art of coffee-making. All told, it is a very good read.

—Mira and Tony Roca, authors of
Memories of Eden

A Muslim on the Bridge doesn't only reflect the voices of moderate middle-class Arab Muslims, it also echoes the voices of many Arab Christians as well as the other minorities in the region. The book's touching stories dynamically weave threads for an honest account hardly found in the mainstream media.

—Fadi Zaghmout, Jordanian blogger and author of
Arous Amman (Amman Bride)

A fascinating, poignant look at a life straddling two different worlds, Iraq and the modern, Western world. Ali's story also tells us what life in Iraq was like long before the U.S. invasion, from his childhood education, his time in the military, and how he watched the divide among secular and religious Muslims growing in intensity. A decade of news-watching could never provide the insight in the pages of this book.

—Michael Luongo, editor,
Gay Travels in the Muslim World

Ali Shakir has written a very personal book. He shares with his readers puzzling encounters with religion in the contemporary historical context. *A Muslim on the Bridge* is a fascinating mosaic of lived Islam that goes beyond the stereotypical representations of the Muslim religion. This testimony of a Muslim in the "grey zone" is a must-read for all those who strive for a more nuanced understanding of Islam in the modern world.

—Dietrich Jung, Prof. in Contemporary Middle East Studies, University of Southern Denmark

A Muslim on the Bridge

On Being an Iraqi-Arab Muslim in the Twenty-First Century

BY
ALI SHAKIR

SIGNAL 8 PRESS
HONG KONG

A Muslim on the Bridge:
On Being an Iraqi-Arab Muslim in the Twenty-First
Century

By Ali Shakir
Published by Signal 8 Press
An imprint of Typhoon Media Ltd
Copyright 2013 Ali Shakir
ISBN: 978-988-15542-9-1

Typhoon Media Ltd:
Signal 8 Press | BookCyclone |Lightning Originals
Hong Kong
www.typhoon-media.com

Cover design: Cristian Checcanin

Due to the sensitive nature of the stories told within the
following scenes, the real names of some of the characters, as well as some of the details surrounding them,
have been changed.

LIGHT UPON LIGHT...
(24. 35)

It is to you.

Contents

Foreword...13

Chapter 1: Hues and Shades.................................17
Chapter 2: Confessions at the Peace Table.....................35
Chapter 3: Living under the Sniper's Gaze.....................57
Chapter 4: "You Are Divorced!".................................71
Chapter 5: On Being Different.................................91
Chapter 6: The Patriarch's Conversion.........................113
Chapter 7: Golden Domes, Secret Prisons,
        and Sticky Sweets.....................................121
Chapter 8: Try a Free Sample of Religion!.....................153
Chapter 9: No Halal Bacon on Board............................165
Chapter 10: Into the Garden...................................181
Chapter 11: What's under the Garment of Piety?...............215
Chapter 12: An Unfavorable Yoke...............................231
Chapter 13: Hadith..249

Works Cited...291
Author's Note...295

Foreword

Ever since I was a child in Baghdad, I have been fascinated by color. Like all children, I loved to draw while lying on the floor, floating in a pond of large sheets of paper, surrounded by watercolors, poster colors, crayons, pencils, pens, brushes, and plastic palettes. Such was my small, happy world. Two decades later, I took up painting as a full-time profession. This only lasted a few years, but even so, and even though it's been a long time since I last painted, colors never cease to surprise me. I still remember the excitement that washed over me when I played with them and my puzzlement at their ambiguous signals.

When I added white to the red, yellow, and blue on my palette, each mixture developed a tint that was neither white nor the original color. The more I repeated the process, the more new, different shades appeared. Little did I know then that my experiments with color would many years later help me understand the way I perceived my religion, Islam. Nevertheless, my brain kept the data crude and un-interpreted until 2001. Appalled by the intensity of the attacks on New York City, I couldn't believe my ears when I heard that they had been planned and executed by Arabs, Muslim men. For a moment, I imagined myself trapped in one of the planes as it pierced the World Trade Center tower and disintegrated into a massive ball of flame. Why would a

Muslim do that? Why would any sane person do something so atrocious?

During that time of turmoil, I recalled my childhood playing with colors. I thought if the white on my plastic palette stood for religion, or any other dogma, for that matter, then the red, yellow, and blue stood for *us*, for people. The outcome of the meeting between white—which cannot be seen when put alone on a blank canvas—and color is outstandingly diverse because although white is constant, colors are not. This realization made me understand why bin Laden's Islam was so different from mine, or from that of Malcolm X, and why Mother Teresa's Christianity was different from George W. Bush's version. It also made me see that my faith has always fluctuated. My Islam now as a man in his forties is very different from my Islam as a child or an adolescent. Only God knows what it will be like when I'm fifty or sixty.

So many books have been written about Islam. After 9/11, the whole world hungered to understand the religion of the man who had given the United States of America its worst day ever. I've read several of those books and found most of them quite interesting, but something is missing. While some writers defend Islam fervently, others viciously attack it. Both groups seem confident in their judgments and conclusions; they both claim to have all the answers, reminding me of a Catholic priest I met once who insisted that there would never be peace in this world unless all Muslims were to become Christians (Catholics, in particular), even if that meant converting one quarter of the world's population.

Amid this global crescendo of conflicting theses—the detractors and supporters, the anti- and pro-Islam—the voice of lay Muslims has gotten lost. No one talks about the Muslims who have a lot of questions and who are not convinced by the clergy's answers. Or, to go back to my analogy of colors again, no one cares to listen to the Muslims in the grey zone—the ones who, in the face of daily challenges and the absence of a clear vision, had no other choice but to improvise. Muslims like myself.

A few years ago, I thought it might be time to lay bare my confusion. Whether I like it or not, religion has permeated my life. Its presence is too palpable to be ignored, so I have decided to talk about it. One final disclaimer, though: it is said that a good writer should steer clear of subjectivity, but I want this book to be subjective through and through. In the following pages, I've poured out my stories and confusion; my feelings; questions; and the choices I've made or, in many cases, failed to make. This is my testimony. These are my confessions.

CHAPTER 1

Hues and Shades

AND WHEN THEY COMMIT OBSCENITY, THEY
WOULD SAY: SO WE FOUND OUR FATHERS
DOING AND SO GOD HAS COMMANDED US TO
DO. SAY: GOD COMMANDS NOT OBSCENITY.
DO YOU SAY OF GOD WHAT YOU KNOW NOT?
(7.28)

More than fourteen centuries ago in Mecca, a land-mark city in the heart of the Arabian Peninsula where Abraham built the Ka'ba, or the House of God, at a spot said to have been marked by angels, Islam was born.

During that time, people used to circle the Ka'ba the way Muslim pilgrims do today, or almost. The ancient Meccans carried out the sacred rite indecently: they circled the House of God naked!

The above verse is believed to have instructed the early Muslims to renounce the pagan heritage of their ancestors. Nudity was banned at the holy place once and for all, yet the influence of pre-Islamic cultures on the doctrine remains a source of controversy to this day.

Scene One

I don't think I will ever be able to forget what happened that evening. I still remember every single detail: the silence, the heaviness in the air—or was it hovering death that weighed the air down? I really don't know, but I remember that it felt exceptionally heavy. I was the night-shift guard at the gateway of the engineering unit where I spent my months of military service. I had just graduated from university and was having a hard time adjusting to military life. I kept myself amused by counting down the remaining days until my discharge.

Luckily, Iraq wasn't at war then. Saddam had lost the war in 1991, and we were still suffering from the aftermath of defeat. It was a tough time for everyone, but if there was a silver lining to the ordeal, it was probably the reduction of the mandatory military service term for university graduates to eighteen months only. Before the defeat in Kuwait, there had been no maximum term, no specified end-point. I carried an old Kalashnikov and stood in a small cabin at the barbed-wire gate waiting for the long, dull hours of my shift to end. As though it was thriving on my ennui, time went by with sadistic slowness.

The hospital next to our unit was a large modern building, quite impressive from the outside. But that wasn't the case inside: all medical services in Iraq had deteriorated badly over the last two years, and many patients died every day. I was standing in the cabin by the gate that day when a doctor or a nurse broke bad news to a poor family. Their young son was dead. I've heard many people cry before, but the wailing of those men and women was completely different. What started out as groaning soon escalated to piercing screams that muted all other sounds. At that moment, it occurred to me that the whole universe was listening to their wounded voices, bowing its head in shame and remorse.

I stood there motionless, no longer an observer of their pain; I *became* their pain. If death had ever had an anthem, this was it. But voices alone fell short of expressing their fury. One of the men picked up a rock from the side of the road and split his own head open. Fresh blood spurted out and sprayed red lines down his pale robe. I felt dizzy and couldn't stand the sight of it, so I closed my eyes and leaned against the cabin wall. My body was soaked in a cold sweat. I thought I was going to faint, but I didn't.

When I opened my eyes, I saw something totally unexpected. One of the women grabbed the collar of her gown and tore it open, exposing her breasts to everyone on the street. The other women followed suit and started to beat their naked chests so hard that they turned purple with bruises. My jaw dropped. It was my first time seeing Iraqi women's breasts revealed in public. I wiped the sweat from my face with my sleeve. When they had first arrived on the scene, I could barely see any of their faces. They walked behind the men, holding the edges of their black cloaks under their chins to prevent them from opening or slipping down. But now they were standing in the middle of the road, hair uncovered and half naked while their torn clothes hung loose from their waists.

Another man took out a gun and started shooting

bullets in the air, the villagers' way of venting their feelings in sadness and in joy. They still do that at weddings and funerals. I had seen Saddam do it on several occasions on television. The women sat in one big circle, yowling and throwing dirt on their scratched faces and bare chests. They stayed like that for about an hour until their shrieks settled down into faint groans again. As darkness fell, they all left.

I drove back home feeling sick. Although we were all Iraqi Muslims, it felt as if we belonged to two different worlds. I couldn't sleep that night. I took sleeping pills, and when that didn't work, I ran to the shower and doused myself with cold water.

Scene Two

When my father told me that his friend Dr. Khaled had passed away, I was dismayed. I felt sad of course for the man and his family, but I was even more upset for the agony-packed days of mourning awaiting me, and all the nonsense they would entail. I've never been fond of social duties, but attending mourning sessions, out of all other obligations, was what I loathed most.

I was fortunate to have been excused from this until I was twenty or so. Even then, I still had the luxury of being selective about it; I went where I wanted to go and met the people I wanted to meet. My father and elder brother had been representing the family most competently, and my occasional appearance with them would only mean that we were extra concerned about the other family—an additional cordiality, so to speak. All that changed when my brother left the country and I had to step up to fill his place beside my father. I no longer had a choice.

Two separate sessions were set up shortly after the funeral procession: one for the women—at the family house—and another for men at the large reception hall annexed to Al Buniya mosque. In times of economic prosperity, both sessions would last for seven days and seven nights. But after years of war, death has become our daily bread in Iraq. The prolonged mourning sessions have thus shrunk, rarely exceeding three days. Which can still be very expensive.

Many mourning halls in Baghdad are furnished with black or brown faux-leather sofas placed against the walls. In the more crowded sessions, parallel rows of rented plastic chairs and tables, each with an ashtray on top, fill the middle of the space. Well-off families, as was the case with Dr. Khaled's, use sterling-silver cups for serving bitter coffee to the consolers, fragrant incense and rose water to perfume their hands, and famous brands of cigarettes, carefully arranged on hand-carved silver trays for the smokers. Instead of playing recorded recitations, they hire renowned reciters to read the Koran at their events. Several prominent reciters are blind—they have memorized whole chapters of the book by heart. They usually arrive at the mosque with young assistants who sit next to them to take care of technical and financial matters.

I heard the blind reciter's voice as I approached the entrance. No handshakes were expected upon arrival. I picked a seat and made myself visible to the grieving family, standing by the door. Before sitting, I offered a short, silent prayer to the soul of the deceased, followed by an audible *Amen*, while wiping my face with the palms of my hands. And then came the most annoying part.

Right before my buttocks touched the chair, I had to rise again as if pricked by a needle. Somewhere between sitting and standing, while rotating the torso in different directions, I was obliged to salute everyone in the hall with the right hand slightly touching my temple, in almost a military way. For someone with poor synchronization skills, this gesture was too much yoga to undergo. I nodded at my neighbors and sat down quietly instead.

Hardly anyone in the hall paid attention to the blind reciter. There was a large cloud of smoke hovering over our heads, and bursts of laughter interrupted the manly chatter every once in a while. Coffee, cigarettes, and chitchats with friends, all for free—what more could men ask for? Everyone seemed to be enjoying his time. Grief was a mere background extra.

The women's mourning session wasn't much different from the men's, my mother later told me. The Koran recitation, the bitter coffee, smoking, and chitchat were typical there too. Dr. Khaled's family placed a mattress on the floor for his bereaved wife, daughters, and sisters to sit on and cry. The other women kneeled to embrace them and cry together or whimper aloud. The abandoning of chairs was meant to show how deeply grieved the family was. And the more tears were shed, the better the family name was honored.

Iraqi widows wear black clothes for months, even years. I knew some ladies who wore black for the rest of their lives.

Two grand dinner banquets were thrown on the third and final night: one for the men at the mosque and another for the women. The open buffets with incredible amounts of food were necessary for wrapping up the ceremony and maintaining family pride in excellence. A five-star hotel catered the feast with waiters in uniforms and exquisite cutlery, china, and glassware. For us Arabs, pride is the best investment we can ever make. It's money very well spent.

Time for the final act, another challenge to my poor multi-tasking skills. After repeating the entry silent prayer, my father and I shook hands with the male members of Dr. Khaled's family, "kissed" them on their cheeks without making actual contact, and murmured a few cliché condolences. My father easily orchestrated his gestures, but it was impossible for me to do both the kissing and the talking. I could either kiss or talk, not both. On my way to the car, my mind calculated the mistakes I'd made during the evening. Unfortunately, there were plenty of them.

Scene Three

Every year on the Prophet's birthday, mystics demonstrated supernatural powers in Adhamiya, a district in northwest Baghdad. I was still in high school when a friend of mine told me about the spectacle. We promised ourselves that we'd watch them together the next year. Indeed, a year later, on the Prophet's birthday, my friend and I were walking through the streets of Adhamiya. As if the whole neighborhood had come out to celebrate the occasion, candles were lit at every doorway and small, colorful flags hung across the streets.

The sound of hymns from distant speakers resonated splendidly through the serpentine alley. For a moment, I thought we must have gotten lost. It was dark and there was no sign of any performance. My friend seemed pretty confident, so I just followed his lead, and we finally reached the venue at a small four-way intersection surrounded by old traditional houses. Everything was well prepared, and the space, usually dark at that time of night, had been illuminated for the show. I heard the faint rhythm of drums in the distance. The beating grew louder and louder, echoing through my chest. Young men with braids slightly above their shoulders, dressed in white gowns, beating drums, and waving huge green flags (green is believed to have been the Prophet's favorite color) turned up.

Except for the dozens of light bulbs that hung over us in a glowing web, there was hardly any other reminder of the twentieth century. I felt a sudden detachment from reality. The way those men looked and dressed took us back in time to the early years of Islam. The surrounding architecture seemed to fit perfectly too. The mystics sat on low cushions around a large carpet. The audience stood watching and listening to the singing and drumming that continued until the real show began.

A young performer stood up, took off his turban, and walked to face another man who was holding a brick between his hands. Complete silence fell over the crowd.

In a flash, he bent forward and hit the brick hard with his forehead, splitting it into two pieces. Everyone cheered and applauded. The mystic smiled timidly and went back to his seat. My heart raced at the sight of blood oozing out of his head. He wiped it off with a piece of cloth and seemed to be doing perfectly well. I sighed.

A couple of men walked into the middle of the ring. One of them held a block of wood firmly against the other's back. I had no idea what was going to happen next, and didn't dare speculate. A third mystic carrying a long sword approached the two men. He unsheathed his sword and waved it in the air before everyone's eyes. The polished blade gleamed and shimmered, reflecting the light of the bulbs on our faces. I thought, *Oh no, not blood again!*

When the swordsman set the point of the blade against the first man's abdomen, we held our breath, and before we knew it, the swordsman had stabbed him. The sword slowly penetrated the man's body like a skewer spears a fresh piece of meat. There wasn't a single expression of pain on his face. Moreover, a ghost of a smile hung on his dry lips. When the assistants removed the wooden block, meant to prevent him from retreating, we saw the sword's tip coming out of his back. There was blood on both ends. It wasn't a trick, either: we really saw it. The sword was still inside the young man when everything suddenly grew dark. I was fainting. My friend, standing right next to me, held my arms and pulled me aside, where I gradually regained consciousness.

Applause roared again. The stabbed man's eyes were open now.

"Thank God he's not dead," I muttered under my breath.

The assistants pressed white towels on his wounds as the swordsman waved the bloodstained blade in the air. No longer shimmering, the sword was dead metal again.

"Breathtaking acts are yet to come," my excited neighbor said.

Not sure I could take any more of this, I took a taxi back home. Supernatural? Absolutely, and overwhelming too. But not so religious. In fact, I still don't know why the so-called mystics had chosen the Prophet's birthday to give their annual show.

When I mentioned that to a Moroccan friend online, he said such practices were very popular in his country. People there considered them to be manifestations of God's ultimate power.

"That's not what we think here," another friend from Saudi Arabia commented. "They are strictly banned. If a man were caught doing those things, he would probably be sentenced to death."

Scene Four

The Baghdadi school of Koran recitation is quite significant in the Islamic world, and it can be easily distinguished from other provincial schools. Our local music and *Maqam* singing imbue the reading with deep poignancy, somewhat converting it into a chanting of laments. This interaction can also be observed in Malaysia, Turkey, and the Muslim countries in North Africa. Traditional music and songs have left their fingerprints on Koran recitations and the call to prayer, just as regional arts have influenced the architecture of mosques. Diverse cultural backgrounds give each one an architectural identity of its own, with the integral domes and minarets differing impressively from one country to another.

Variety, however, is not limited to arts and architecture. For years I thought there were only two types of Islamic prayers, Sunni and Shia. The most obvious difference between them would be the position of the arms. While Shia keep their arms to the sides, Sunnis crossed them over their chests or slightly above the navel. Only by chance, and while discussing prayer with a friend whose mother was Syrian, I realized that some of my beliefs were mistaken.

Sarmad had spent much of his childhood years in Damascus, where he'd learned to pray the Sunni way. I too had been taught Sunni prayer in my elementary school in Baghdad. When we prayed at the mosque, we performed exactly the same movements and uttered the same Koranic verses. As for the supplication, which should be repeated silently during the seated part in the middle and at the end of prayer, neither Sarmad nor I knew that we'd been reading two different versions. And it wasn't just a word or two: actually, there were considerable differences between the two texts. This was quite a discovery for both of us. *I wonder what other hidden differences there are,* I remember thinking.

Scene Five

When he came back from a weekend trip to Germany, Ali, my childhood friend and namesake—a civil engineer who had been living and working in London—was subjected to a lengthy interrogation on arrival at the airport. "Why did you go to Germany? Where did you stay? What were you doing there?" After endless repetitions of the same questions and answers, Ali was finally fed up. He unzipped his handbag, took out the porn DVD he'd bought in Berlin, and put it down on the officer's desk. "Look! Do you see what I have here? You really needn't be afraid of me. Just because I have an Arabic name and was born in a Muslim country, that doesn't make me a terrorist. I'm not!" The officer smiled, and with typical British reservedness told Ali that he never said he was a terrorist. He did let him go after seeing the DVD, nonetheless.

Whatever the officer's true intentions may have been, I think Ali made a very good point (even if I don't agree with his means of proving it). Saying someone is a Muslim hardly tells anything about the human he or she is. It doesn't say if he's an extremist, a mystic, a secular person, or even an atheist who's being called a Muslim simply and only because he was born to Muslim parents. It's a vague statement that hardly gives any guidance, like introducing someone by saying they're from the Northern or Southern Hemisphere. We tend to forget that every label is but a vast spectrum that consists of millions of different individuals with different—and sometimes conflicting—views of life.

Scene Six

I didn't know it at the time, but the images I saw through the taxi window on my way to the airport would be my last of the city where I was born and had spent much of my life. The streets, the palm trees, and the Tigris River... everything seemed so poignant. Thinking I was only going to be gone for a month, I had barely enough clothing items in my suitcase to survive winter. When the plane landed in Amman, Jordan, the city felt like heaven: a steady flow of electricity and water; no hours of lining up at gas stations for fuel; and most importantly, no car explosions, suicide bombers, or abductions—the lethal banalities of postwar Iraq. Amman seemed like an oasis of peace where I could walk safely down the streets at any given time, day or night. And walk I did.

Every single day, no matter whether it rained or snowed, I walked for hours on end. One month followed another, and another. With harrowing news about the worsening situation in Iraq, the prospect of my return to Baghdad seemed to evaporate. I stayed in Jordan for two and a half years. Even when I left Amman in 2008, I still had to go back every now and then to deal with family issues. On one of those visits, I read a newspaper article about a public meeting with Indian spiritual leader Sri Sri Ravi Shankar.

The guru had arrived in Jordan after a short visit to Baghdad, where he'd given healing courses to groups of traumatized Iraqis of different sects. Until then, I hadn't heard the man's name and knew absolutely nothing about his courses and his foundation, The Art of Living. I was impressed, though, that he'd risked going to Iraq at a critical time to help the victims of violence, and I couldn't pass up the opportunity to hear his account of the trip. I arrived early at the Sheraton Hotel's grand ballroom and sat close to the podium. In less than half an hour, the room was packed to the rafters. The audience of mainly Jordanians, but also Arabs and foreigners, teemed with anticipation for *Guruji*—as his dedicated followers loved to call him.

I was interested to learn more about the courses and their relaxing properties. It struck me, though, that not a single person in the room was communicating in Arabic. Some spoke flawless English, so much so that I thought they were British. But when they started discussing local matters, a few Arabic words escaped their lips, enough to make me realize they were actually native Jordanians. I was baffled. I listened to the ladies behind me as they talked about the expensive American school in which they had enrolled their little children. Although they tried to conceal it, their accent was so obvious. When they couldn't find the right English words, they used Arabic synonyms, and then swiftly switched back to English, making horrible grammar mistakes along the way. I wondered, *What's wrong with using Arabic, their mother tongue?* I couldn't fathom why an Arab would communicate with another Arab through a foreign language neither of them had mastered.

The room rang with applause when the speaker arrived. Sri Sri talked about his mission in Iraq and worldwide. His foundation was teaching a special breathing technique that helped—or so they claimed—to eliminate daily stress. He then took some time to answer questions from the audience, and at the end of the evening we all did a short guided meditation. As I walked back to my hotel, I wondered whether I was so different from the audience at the Amman Sheraton ballroom: I too expressed myself in English occasionally. So if a passerby heard me one day, would they think I was inauthentic, exactly the way I had thought of the ladies behind me?

Scene Seven

Bewildered, I watched millions of Iraqi Shia on television as they marched to their holy shrines on Ashoura Day—the anniversary of the martyrdom of the Prophet's grandsons in Karbala, in southern Iraq. During his years in power, Saddam had strictly banned the ritual. But when he was gone, it came back more passionate than ever. The penitents brutally beat themselves until their bodies bled. I couldn't understand why people would willingly torture themselves like that. If these weeping men and women were my people, then how come I felt so estranged from them? It wasn't the first time I had asked myself this question.

The way my siblings and I were raised was quite different from the way the majority of Iraqi parents raised their children. At the age of five, I was taught to sing "Old MacDonald Had a Farm," "London Bridge Is Falling Down," "Roly Poly," and the French "Frère Jacques." I learned the English ABCD in kindergarten before I learned the Arabic alphabet in elementary school. And while I used a knife and fork to cut the food on my plate, thinking it was the natural way to eat, thousands of Iraqi children my age sat on the floor and used their bare hands to eat rice and okra stew from a single plate that served the entire family. When they had meat, they devoured it and would not let go of the small pieces until they had eaten every last bit right down to the bones, and sucked the marrow too. No cutlery, napkins, or tablecloth were necessary. In many cases, there were not even tables.

No, I wasn't born into a rich, aristocratic family. My parents—like thousands of young, educated, middle-class Iraqis—had chosen to lead a Westernized lifestyle because it was the trend at the time they got married. When I joined the army, I first realized how encapsulated I was. Being abruptly uprooted from my comfortable, hybrid ghetto and forced to mingle with people with whom I had very little, if anything, in common was disorienting. I found a couple of hybrid friends like myself there, but we felt lonely and isolated from the rest of our mates.

I kept my mouth shut most of the time, lest I make a stupid remark on religion that could have irritated someone or hurt their feelings. I also pretended to have a stomach ulcer and lived on water and bread alone because I couldn't eat any of the food served to us at the camp. I think I managed to deceive everyone, but I wasn't happy. While my mates clearly belonged to the land, I felt I didn't belong anywhere. I was a cheap replica, a parasite.

"Mama, Mama!" my brother called our mother while we were playing one day. A poor rural woman who had been cleaning our house then was down on her knees scrubbing the floor. I saw her smile and say under her breath, "Mama? Let's see what happens when you grow up and your friends in the army hear you say that!" She thought I didn't hear her, but I did. Her own children never called her Mama. Most likely, they called her *Youm*, or *Youmma*—the native equivalents of the word. She was a simple illiterate woman, but very astute. I remembered her quip twenty years later. Indeed. There was absolutely no way my brother or I could have referred to our mother during our military service as *Mama*.

The Muslims on the Bridge

It's not new to me. I've felt like a stranger most of my life. More so in Baghdad than now in Amsterdam, Omar, an Iraqi dentist, said as we chatted online. He, his wife, and their two children had been admitted as refugees in Holland. Omar's words didn't surprise me because I knew exactly what he meant. Over the years, I've met and talked with many Arab Muslims like us, who not only spoke, dressed, and ate differently from the majority of people in their own countries. Most importantly, they/we also *thought* differently.

I sometimes envy the Muslims who don't feel the need to question their faith, its teachings, and its rules. I wish I could allow my mind to indulge in the comfort of total submission. But my mind doesn't work like that. It's been trained to reason and argue, and there is no button I can press to switch it off. It's a big problem in our part of the world, where it is risky for thoughts, opinions, and ideas not to conform to mainstream values and standards. But what if those standards and values are wrong? The question has often left me perplexed and feeling like I'm standing on a bridge—a frail suspension bridge, shaking in the wind.

My only consolation is that I'm not alone. There are so many of us out there. We are neither accepted by our own people, whose blood, physical features, and language we share, nor will we ever be fully welcomed by the people on the other side, whose thinking and lifestyle we're more familiar with. East and West. The seventh century and the twenty-first century. Torn between two different affiliations and times that combat inside and outside of us, the bridge has become our mandatory buffer zone.

When I last left Baghdad in 2006, more than a dozen bridges—several of which had been closed for security reasons—connected the banks of the Tigris. A year later, a suicide truck bomb exploded on the oldest one and brought it down. I had passed by that bridge on my way to the airport. It felt very refreshing and soothing, and I often marveled at how pretty the city looked from there. I try to think positively about my metaphorical bridge position too. *Maybe from where I'm standing I can have a better view and understanding of both banks/ worlds,* I sometimes tell myself. I've always loved driving and walking across bridges. Maybe *living* on a bridge is not so bad after all.

CHAPTER 2

Confessions at the Peace Table

HE SAID: FORGIVE ME MY LORD, AND GRANT ME DOMINION WHICH SHALL NOT BE TO ANYONE AFTER ME, FOR YOU ARE THE ULTIMATE BESTOWER.

(38.35)

In this verse, King Solomon made an exception to a rule. Of all the prophets mentioned in the Koran, he was the only one who dared approach God with such a worldly and selfish, yet genuinely human, request. Solomon's wish was indeed granted. His Lord gave him exactly what he wanted, and what we all yearn for: power.

Scene One

I have never been able to stomach the concept of original sin. If it was Adam's fault, why, should I spend a lifetime paying off his debt? I didn't ask him to sin; I wasn't even there when he did it! Thankfully, as a Muslim, I don't have to because the Koran's account of the incident is quite different from the Bible's. After being expelled from heaven, Adam repented for his sin wholeheartedly, and God accepted his repentance. The file was closed once and for all, and a new chapter started. The Koran also says no man shall be held accountable for the mistakes of another. Each of us is fully responsible for our own actions, good or bad, and will be rewarded or punished accordingly. This makes a lot of sense to me, but does it mean Islam is a guilt-free religion? Far from it.

I honestly don't know whether guilt is an innate component of faith or was infused into it later on. It sometimes occurs to me that the clergy are keen on blaming us because blame and rebuke keep them employed. It's their full-time job and it pays very well. They want us to feel guilty all the time, and we actually do. Guilt has become such an integral part of our psyche that we miss it when it's gone (if it ever leaves). Rarely have I listened to a Friday sermon free from reproach. There always seems to be something wrong with us, something to regret doing, or not doing.

"We must celebrate calamities when they strike us," the preachers often tell us. The messengers of God rejoiced in suffering and asked to be put to even harsher tests. We should therefore resent comfort and curb our carnal desires like they did, for we are not truly religious until we've totally abstained from our lusts. But is that even plausible? I attempted to emulate that model during my childhood and early adolescence: I wanted to attain the devotion and endurance of Abraham, Job, Moses, Jesus, and Mohammed. Alas, I couldn't. My anger would burst out at the smallest mishaps. I often questioned God and felt terribly guilty about it after my anger subsided.

"Many of you pray for God to send you money, a beautiful wife, sons and daughters, or victory against your enemies," the imam in our neighborhood mosque said in one of his weekly sermons. "You ought to be ashamed of yourselves. These things are the husk of life. Instead, you should ask for patience, wisdom, and piety," he angrily chided us from his high platform. *But if God didn't mind Solomon's request, why should He mind mine?* I couldn't understand. If He is aware of our weaknesses, why would He be disgusted by us when we confess them to Him? Maybe God saw Solomon's admission of imperfection as praise to His perfection.

Scene Two

I've spent more than half of my life trying to survive wars and their later consequences—which can be much worse than the wars themselves. I was only eleven when the Iraqi-Iranian war broke out. And at the age of thirty-seven, when I last left Baghdad, the city was on the verge of a ruthless civil conflict. No matter what war-planners say to legitimize them, I can say from my long experience that no war is ever just. All wars are unfair and futile too. They create more problems than solutions, but there's nothing like them to boost the politicians' egos, so they go on making up excuses to justify dragging us into more of them. And if they are good at it, we believe them.

When we are at war, we only think of survival. Not until a war is over do we see the realize the actual damage. In military wars, however, we can escape the bombing by hiding in bunkers. They may not be completely safe, but they offer some protection. In the wars that rage inside of us, within our souls, there is no protection whatsoever. I've been through both types of wars, internal and external. It took me long years before coming to terms with the gap between what *should be* and what *is*. Torn between unrealistic heavenly ideals and my tangible earthly needs, I had unconsciously split myself in two: I was two men living in one body, and neither one was happy.

The ferocity of the last war forced me to reflect on life, others' and mine. It was as if a black curtain had dropped away to show me the falsity of many things I had hitherto deemed vital, and the profundity of other things I had taken for granted or even ignored. People were dying by the thousands, and the survivors' hopes and dreams were wiped out in mere seconds. Tired of conflict, gasping for peace and freedom, I finally dared to unlock the dark, forbidden cellar of my being where I had been keeping my hatred, arrogance, jealousy, greed, and vengeance. I wasn't willing to remove anything, though; I just let light and fresh air in, and left to sort out a few other things. But I didn't lock the door behind me, either.

Scene Three

Everyone talked about balance with such admiration when I was growing up that—without knowing the word's meaning—it soon became a part of my regular vocabulary. Even the Koran mentions it on several occasions. In the chapter Al-Rahman (The Beneficent), God says He imposed balance in the universe immediately after creating heaven and earth.

Like all children, I wanted to impress my parents: I wanted to become a poised, well-balanced man. I remember being patted on the head for saying that, but I wondered what it actually meant to be balanced. Was a balanced man someone who avoided controversy and abided by the old ways? Was he someone who pretended to be perfect even if he knew he was not, just to get a pat on the back?

A couple of years ago, I looked the word up in several dictionaries. *Balance* was *equipoise between contrasting, opposing, or interacting elements*, the Merriam-Webster online dictionary said. Does this mean we cannot possibly be in balance unless we first experience our extremes? After pondering the definition, I became convinced this is what it implies. Birth and death, day and night, happiness and sadness: remarkable antitheses manifest themselves in our lives all the time, but we don't pay them much attention.

A realization hit me: *No wonder good and evil are so intertwined inside of me. I am a reflection of this universe, after all.* I also realized that I owed so much to the ambiguous, fighting voices in my head. Anger, for one, has been a motivator for painting and writing, and fear has saved my life many times too. When I had this realization, I decided my Dr. Jekyll and Mr. Hyde needed to become friends. I gathered my extremes around the peace table to sign a memorandum of understanding based on acceptance, openness, and mutual respect. *War is over*, I declared. I'm afraid there is very little I can do to ease the suffering of the people in Iraq, and I have no clue how long the violence will last there. My main concern right now is to keep my hard-earned inner peace accord intact. I know it won't be easy, but setting the goal alone has, in a very special way, made me feel balanced.

Scene Four

I watched a captured insurgent confessing on television. Bursting with fury, he carried his gun, willing to kill everyone in his way. Military, civilian, young, old, male, female, adult, or child, it really didn't matter. He was told everyone was a legitimate target, and he believed it. Had the sheikh told him to blow himself up, he would have unhesitatingly obeyed. The imam at the mosque had assured him that as a martyr, he could look forward to the special treatment that martyrs received in heaven: beautiful virgins; garments of pure silk; delicious fruits; rivers of milk, honey, and wine that flowed through mansions crafted from gold and gems. He couldn't wait to go there to experience the justice he had never had in this world.

During and after the war in 2003, thousands of insurgents sneaked through our unwatched borders to make our lives hell. Some came from Iran; others from Syria, Saudi Arabia, and Jordan. On their websites and in their homemade videos, they chanted Islamic and patriotic slogans against the American invaders. But in reality, they were killing more and more Iraqis every day. We heard their gunshots at night and explosions during the day.

I never saw one of these insurgents in person, however. They seemed like ghosts to me, which piqued my curiosity about them even more. I wanted to know what they were thinking and how they could so cold-bloodedly murder people they didn't know. The broadcast confessions of the captured insurgent on television did answer some of my questions, but there were still many more unanswered. Had someone paid them to do it? Did they volunteer to kill? What could possibly be a fair price for suicide? A million dollars? Two? Were they fully conscious when they pressed the button or pulled the trigger, or were they sedated beforehand? Ever since my childhood, when I first heard about the operations executed by the Palestinian Fedayeen, I've had those questions in the back of my mind.

I knew Israel had been subjugating them, confiscating their lands and denying them their basic rights. I watched their suffering on television every night, and it distressed me badly. I wasn't sure, though, if the Palestinians' righteous cause could justify the Fedayeen's killing of civilians or hijacking of airplanes. How was it supposed to ease their people's pain and solve their urgent problems? It was far too late to ask my naïve questions, anyway. Jihad—which translates as *struggle* in Arabic—is an acclaimed tradition in the decades-long conflict. Thousands of Palestinian babies have been (and are still being) named after it.

During the Second World War, the Nazis exploited Arabs' religious sentiments against Jewish settlement in Palestine and the Allied Powers by reviving the ancient notion of jihad. This was done with blessings from the then Grand Mufti of Jerusalem and influential nationalist Amin Al Husseini, as well as his personal friend and founder of the Muslim Brotherhood in Egypt, Hassan Al Banna. But like most religious motifs, jihad too can be viewed at more than one level. While Sufis understand it as a spiritual quest to transcend man's evil inclinations and desires, more radical Islamist groups have adopted a rather linear perspective that defines jihad as a holy war against all non-Muslims, and Muslim deviates too.

The violent version, however, became increasingly popular after the mullahs succeeded in converting Iran from a secular monarchy to a strict Shia theocracy in 1979. They dedicated much of their country's rich resources to export their revolution to the Arab and Muslim world, prompting Saudi Arabia to respond by funding Sunni fundamentalism. The rivalry between the two Islamic poles coincided with the Soviet invasion of Afghanistan and the rise of the U.S.-funded and armed Islamic resistance there.

In less than thirty years, these generously financed conflicts have by-produced the Taliban, Al Qaeda, Hamas in Palestine, Hezbollah in Lebanon, and any number of militias in Iraq and other Islamic countries. My late self-reconciliation didn't change my mind. I strongly believe that terrorism cannot be justified. It can and should be better understood, though. Instead of judging, which is the easiest thing to do, I started tracing root causes and putting more emphasis on the what, how, and why. The answers I found have made all the difference.

Scene Five

Up until the early eighties, there was not a single covered teacher in my school. I actually can't recall any girl with *hijab* in our neighborhood either. And except for the very few men who'd grown their beards like hippies, there were hardly any other bearded men in our area. My parents did not pray then, and neither did my friends' parents. They didn't fast or go to the mosque and would only read the Koran occasionally. My father used to drink whenever we had guests for dinner. Unlike these days, religion was not even a popular topic of discussion in our house.

When I left Iraq in 2006, the secular lifestyle of the seventies and eighties had totally vanished, and the city scene had shifted to the opposite extreme. Only a few bare-headed women could still be found on the streets, subject to verbal and physical abuse from bearded men who wouldn't hesitate to curse at or even hit them on their heads. Several Christian girls covered their hair (even though this was not a requirement for them) to avoid being distinguished from their Muslim counterparts and targeted by the fanatics. It was a time of great fear for everyone.

Many Muslims today are committed to praying at the mosque, fasting during Ramadan, and reading the Koran. Millions go to Mecca every year; hundreds of millions of Muslim women cover their hair. Paradoxically enough, along with what many Islamists like to call a religious awakening came a terrible increase in crimes like murder, rape, and theft.

"Why is it that when he finally became religious and we all thought he'd change for the better, his behavior became even worse than before?" a sobbing relative of mine complained, and righteously so, about her oldest son who'd abandoned her and his elderly father after a small quarrel. "What use is his religiosity if it makes him such a cruel-hearted man?"

I've personally seen a great deal of evil committed under the cover of Islam. If, for instance, you want to bribe a functionary—most jobs, in many Arab countries, cannot be done without bribes—you will have to approach him or her by saying, "This is just a simple gift. And the Prophet, may peace be upon him, accepted gifts." While your money finds its way to their pockets, the frowns will disappear, replaced by warm and welcoming smiles. Your work will then be finished swiftly because they wouldn't want to be late for prayer.

Less than a month after his wedding, a childhood friend of mine was abducted while on his way home from work. In 2005's total absence of order, the business of abduction boomed in Baghdad. The kidnappers called my friend's family the next day to demand a ransom. They first asked for two hundred thousand American dollars, but after a week of difficult negotiations, they finally settled for twenty thousands. My friend's family paid the money and he was set free. When I went to visit him, I couldn't stop laughing when my friend told me that the abductors, who were Sunni Muslims just like him, had asked for an extra few thousand dollars to do alms.

Scene Six

Architecture school seemed like the perfect place to merge my passion for painting and design, but it was wartime when I finished high school and went to study at Baghdad University. (Then again, it's always wartime in Iraq.) The university campuses were scattered over a vast area that used to be an ancient grove of palm trees by the river. The buildings were designed by the renowned German-American architect Walter Gropius and TAC in the early sixties. Education was and is still free in Iraq, but despite that, our social and financial differences couldn't have been more obvious.

With every design project we were assigned at the university, we had to prepare a series of presentations and undergo evaluations that cost an awful lot of money. Students from well-off families used the finest materials on the market. Some were pampered enough to have German Rotring pens, UHU adhesives, French Canson paper, and English instruments all shipped from abroad. Their final sheets gleamed with rich airbrush colors.

Students from poor families, on the other hand, could barely afford cheap local materials. The morning of the final presentation day, they arrived at the university with red, sore eyes from staying up all night, working on their projects by quivering, dim candlelight. All the power stations in Iraq had been bombed during the war, and the prices of generators were skyrocketing. It was summer then, and Baghdad summers can be suffocating, more so in the absence of electricity. The poor students' sheets had ugly wrinkles and sweat stains all over them after long bus rides to school. Their poorly executed designs only received mediocre appreciation from the jurors despite their (sometimes) original ideas. Let's face it: it wasn't often that destitute students could come up with creative designs. Not with all the pressure and frustration they were under.

In Iraq—as in any country—it was the poor who paid the biggest price of war. Their sons died on the frontlines because unlike the affluent, they couldn't afford to bribe high-ranking officers to assign them to safe residential units. If they had tried to run away, they would have been considered traitors and shot dead on the spot. They lived their lives without hope, much less creativity.

I saw two of my friends turn their backs on religion, reading books on existentialism and drinking the cheapest spirits. It was actually they who introduced me to Herman Hesse's world. "If God doesn't give a damn about me, my dreams, and the way I feel, then there is no point for me to obey His rules either," one of my friends told me. "As if He's only made us to make the rich feel happy with what they've got," he vented his rage at Allah, which was relatively acceptable then. But this wasn't how another friend of ours, Isam, had responded to his frustration.

Nadia was nothing like the girls he had known before. She was pretty and rich, driving her own car in a tight miniskirt, mingling freely with boys in the university and joking with them. Isam was mesmerized by her aggressive beauty and personality. She was the girl of his dreams, but when he finally attempted to approach her, she turned him down at once because he was poor. Isam fell into a deep depression and became indifferent to everything and everyone. After a while, he started showing symptoms of religiosity. Praying and reading Islamic books gave him solace; he was often seen with a number of them under his arm. He lowered his gaze whenever there were girls passing, including Nadia; the girl he most loved. Both in lecture rooms and in life, Isam had decided to take a back seat, for he was certain that there was no place for him in the front row. Well, not unless he forced his way into it.

Two Stories

Somewhere in 1937, a baby boy was born to a destitute single mother in the small and insignificant village of Al-Awja, south of Tikrit. The infant was never to see his father. Gossips whispered that Hussein Al Majid had walked out on his wife while she was pregnant, but the official story says that he died shortly before she gave birth to their child. No one knows exactly who gave the boy his peculiar name, Saddam, one meaning of which is *he who frequently collides*. Either way, his mother remarried shortly after his birth, and Saddam had to endure the most brutal treatment at the hands of his heartless stepfather, who couldn't stand the sight of him.

Constantly beaten and humiliated, Saddam only found

freedom in the wilderness, where he wandered alone, half-naked and hungry. He got his first pleasure from chasing and torturing insects and animals, preparing himself for the next phase of his life, when he would kill people instead. Young Saddam's insatiable appetite for power led him to join the clandestine Ba'ath Party, whose ideology was an Arabic blend of fascism and communism. Originally founded in Syria in 1947, the party had expanded to neighboring Iraq, and its members had a reputation for being totally anti-religious. The ambitious young man from Al-Awja was no exception.

After years of conspiracies and assassinations—at which he always excelled—Saddam became a key figure in the party. And when the Ba'athists finally seized power, he was named vice president. Saddam remained in that position until 1979, when he forced the incumbent president (and his, Saddam's, distant cousin) Ahmed Hassan Al-Bakr to step down. Saddam became the official leader of Iraq, and the rest is history.

The biggest turning point in Saddam's life, however, came after he miraculously survived a gigantic war that left him with a wreck of a country in 1991. The war made him realize that he was no longer America's man in the Middle East. Like expired canned food, he was going to be thrown away, but he wouldn't accept defeat easily.

Everyone was betting against him. We all thought his days were numbered, but to our dismay, his reign lasted another twelve years. When asked once what his favorite book was, Saddam's reply was Machiavelli's *The Prince*.

Indeed, he seems to have made perfect use of every single page of the infamous book. Convinced that the only way out of his dilemma was to play the card of faith, all of a sudden, the once secular-socialist comrade turned religious. He launched a grand campaign to re-Islamize his already-Muslim-majority nation, and declared himself its devout leader.

The president gave orders to build huge mosques throughout the country with his initials engraved on every corner. His wife covered her dyed platinum-blonde hair, and so did all the women comrades in the Ba'ath party. Iraqi television started broadcasting religious programs more frequently. And last but not least, Saddam called for the formation of a mighty military force to liberate the Aqsa Mosque in Jerusalem from the Zionist grip. Not only did his tactics give him extra years in power when he was most vulnerable, but most importantly, they also created a halo around him that would outlive his time. On Saturday, December 30, 2006, dressed in black, Saddam walked calmly to the gallows with a copy of the Holy Koran in his hand. The moment the dictator was executed, in the eyes of many Muslims, a martyr was born.

Back in 1957, when Saddam had just turned twenty, another child was born in Riyadh, Saudi Arabia to a self-made tycoon of Yemeni origin and his Syrian wife. Shortly after Osama's birth, his parents divorced, and his father went on marrying more and more wives. As in modern-day corporations, which periodically lay off useless employees and replace them with more capable ones, when it came to marriage, Mohammed bin Laden strongly believed in competition. Every once in a while, he discharged his old wives to marry younger and prettier girls. Unluckily for Osama's mother, it was her turn now.

There is no precise number for the women bin Laden the father had married during his lifetime. While some rumors have it that he'd married a dozen, others insist that the number had exceeded twenty. But in any case, when Osama was ten years old, his father died in a plane crash, leaving behind more than fifty sons, all carrying a surname that would petrify the entire world after September 11, 2001. I don't know why, but when I read about the bin Laden progeny, I remembered something I had seen many years ago. In his first animated film *Snow White and the Seven Dwarfs*, Walt Disney had decided to name the dwarfs—nameless in the original German fable—after their characteristics: Grumpy, Happy, Sneezy, Sleepy, Dopey, Bashful, and Doc. I think I can now see his point.

I don't know about the bin Ladens, but I reckon Osama's quandary as a child was that no matter how hard he tried to be noticed, especially by his father, his efforts were in vain. He was neither the first child nor the last, and his mother was obviously not his father's favorite wife either. Most likely, it was difficult for Mohammed bin Laden to tell who was who, much less who the child of which wife was. In his crowded colony of sons, daughters, and wives, there was hardly any space of recognition, let alone attention for his seventeenth child Osama.

Soon after the divorce, Osama's mother married a

manager in her ex-husband's company and moved to Jeddah to live with him. Osama joined her there. Unlike Saddam's stepfather, Osama's was not rude at all. He looked after the little boy who seemed to have everything—riches and a prominent family name. But was that enough? In the community where he had grown up, Islam was the dominant force in the lives of the people, and the authority of the clerics was equal to that of politicians. In some cases, it was even greater. Osama saw this and realized that the more commitment to his religion he showed, the more acknowledgment he would receive. If he had failed to attract his father and his family's attention for who he was, Osama was determined now to make them see him through the admiring—or for that matter, petrified—eyes of others.

So much has been said about Al Qaeda's origins, links, and operations that I don't have anything to add here. Whether Osama bin Laden had some hidden agenda or not, it's not really important because the damage has already been done. Millions of Muslims around the world have been stigmatized as terrorists since 2001, and the stereotype is not likely to change anytime soon. But Osama didn't really care: he was busy pursuing his childhood dream and making his own legend. In a video released after his killing in Abbottabad, Pakistan, he is shown sitting on the floor with a remote control in his hand, flicking between the news channels that had been covering one of his notorious speeches. With an unkempt grey beard and a blanket on his shoulders, he rocked back and forth as he watched his image on television. In his fifties, considered the United States of

America's prime enemy, Osama bin Laden was still a child craving attention.

Scene Seven

Due to high birth rates, young adults today make up a large percentage of Arab and Muslim communities. Energy surges through their bodies, looking for an outlet. Everyone around them tells them they should suppress their feelings and desires because they are *aib* (shameful). They are instructed to be religious, as if religion is an antidote to being natural. They spend their days brimming with frustration, disappointment, and anger. Like landmines buried in the sand, they are likely to explode at any given moment.

Not many Arab boys can afford to travel, play football in their gardens, or paint like my brother and I did. And not all young girls can indulge in pop music and romantic novels like my sister had done either. Even in our rather liberal upbringing, we still received a fair share of reproach and *aib*. Sex is restricted to marriage, entertainment is expensive, and opinions and ideas are doomed to be aborted under brutal dictatorships, social and political. Thousands of young Arabs and Muslims graduate from university every year to struggle with unemployment, and millions more are illiterate and can be easily misled. They long to manifest their potential and be appreciated, but all doors are closed. Except for one.

There is no one single reason for terrorism. It would be naïve to think that only poverty is what triggers Islamic violence because neither Osama bin Laden nor his

Egyptian heir Ayman Al-Zawahiri had been poor. Injustice is definitely a major cause, but it's not limited to Arabs and Muslims. Even in the so-called First World, many poor, abused, or desperate young men and women end up being serial killers, drug dealers, prostitutes, or even corrupt politicians. They too stand at the crossroads where Saddam, Osama, Hitler, Stalin, Mussolini, and other criminals and dictators stood before, and they make their same choice: to take revenge. There is one fundamental difference between the two worlds, though. Religion covers no back in the West, and they would be treated as outlaws there, but in our world, if they are smart enough, they can be heroes.

Through the centuries, religion and the state have intertwined and melted into one entity. While it was essential for the sovereigns to be baptized in Islam in order to stay in power, the clergy, on the other hand, needed the ruler's protection to secure their dominance over the masses, much like the bond between the Catholic Church and the royal houses of medieval Europe. The common people, as a result of this courtship, are being suppressed twofold, and the injustice received from politicians and clerics reflects off Muslim males onto their wives, sons, and daughters, completing its circle in the community.

Scene Eight

On December 17, 2010, Mohammed Bouazizi, a twenty-six-year-old street vendor in Tunisia, woke up to the resonating call of sunrise prayer. Just like every other day, he left for work after having a humble breakfast of tea and bread. Mohammed sold fruits and vegetables on a wooden cart he pushed down the streets of his rural town. That day, however, before he had sold anything, a municipal inspector stopped him and insisted he pay a fine for not having a license. Except for a few coins, Bouazizi's pockets were empty. He spent what little money he had earned on maintaining his family's livelihood. The inspector refused to listen to his pleas. She seized his weighing scale and threw away his merchandise, and when he tried to stop her, she slapped him in front of everyone in the street.

As if his mind had stopped working, his hurt took over. He poured fuel on his body and set himself ablaze in front of the people who'd seen him being humiliated and beaten. In that desperate moment, it didn't matter that suicide was one of the gravest sins (if not the gravest) in Islam. Bouazizi could no longer stand the injustices done to him and his family, and taking his own life was his only way of rebelling. Instantly, the story was on almost every blog in Tunisia. Thousands of demonstrators took to the streets, shouting and condemning the repressive regime.

Less than a month after Mohammed Bouazizi's self-immolation, the situation was getting out of control. President Zine El Abidine Ben Ali had no other choice than to flee the country he had ruled for more than thirty years, taking refuge in Saudi Arabia. A dead man toppled a dictator in Tunisia, but that wasn't the end of the story. Less than a month later, another revolution broke out in Egypt. Young Egyptian activists launched a nationwide protest campaign online to bring down Hosni Mubarak's decadent government over the brutal murder of Khaled Saeed, a twenty-eight-year-old man who was tortured to death at the hands of the police in Alexandria. Just a short time after photos of Saeed's deformed corpse were uploaded, they went viral.

Hundreds of thousands of demonstrators responded immediately, gathering in Tahrir Square in Cairo and throughout Egypt. After a couple of weeks of conflict with the security forces, and despite the escalating number of casualties among the protestors, it was obvious that those young men and women were not going to leave empty-handed. When Mubarak finally resigned, other Arab protestors rallied to demand political changes in Libya, Yemen, Bahrain, Syria, Jordan, Oman, Morocco, and even Iraq.

This was unprecedented. It had happened neither in 1988, when Saddam used chemical weapons to kill thousands of Iraqi Kurds in the village of Halabja, nor in 1982, when president Assad the father gave orders to kill other thousands of Syrian civilians in the town of Hama. After news of the two massacres spread, a few condemnations were heard here and there, but that was that. Saddam remained in power for fifteen years afterwards, Assad eighteen. In our remarkably connected world, nevertheless, things seem to work in quite a different way. News, pictures, and videos today travel at the speed of a finger click on a keyboard or a cell phone.

For years it seemed that the Arab dictators had come to stay. Several presidents, including Mubarak, had taken steps towards a hereditary succession of power in their countries. We saw all their plans turn upside down in the blink of an eye, and not even their clergy allies would do a thing to help them. Furthermore, there were voices among the protestors shouting pro-secular slogans. A new age was rising, we mistakenly thought. Now that the winds of change have passed, or almost, it turns out they were blowing in favor of the Islamists whose power has outgrown their need for protection. When the time was right, they stepped up to take the rulers' places in a perfectly democratic manner. Their candidates—relying on the popularity of Islam— won a sweeping majority, alienating the actual planners of change: the liberals, whose performance in parliamentary elections was embarrassingly poor.

"Democracy is not for us," one of my friends grumbled while we were talking about the Arab Spring on the phone. "We all wanted Saddam to go, but look at what happened in Iraq when they ousted him. Arabs are not prepared for democracy." Although I disagree with my friend's passive outlook, I must say I understand his worries about drastic changes because we know from experience how dangerous change can be. As much as I wish it, I don't think there will be a separation between church and state in the Arab world anytime soon. An Islamic renaissance has yet to dawn, and until it does, Islam will continue to grant easy access to authority and power to whomever craves them.

CHAPTER 3

Living under the Sniper's Gaze

YOU ARE THE BEST NATION SENT FOR
MANKIND, ENJOINING BENEFICENCE AND
FORBIDDING MALEVOLENCE, AND BELIEVING
IN GOD.

(3.110)

When the Koran was revealed to Mohammed, the Arabs were worshiping idols crafted of almost every imaginable material. They had gods of stone and wood, and even edible ones made of dates. Many fathers buried their female infants alive immediately after birth as part of a common culture in which women were looked down upon. Greedy usurers lent money to the poor and demanded excessive interest that many failed to pay. They confiscated the borrowers' mules, and sold their sons and daughters into slavery.

Arabian tribes used to conquer and plunder one another. The strong oppressed the weak, and people committed all types of transgressions brazenly. It was time for God to intervene. He could have punished them the way He'd done with the ancient sinners, but He didn't. He chose to send them a prophet instead.

Scene One

After the guests finished eating and watching the belly dancer swing and sway her stocky body to the beat of drums, the bride and groom retired to their new bedroom. The real challenge was yet to begin. The women of their families gathered at the door, clapping and singing, adding to their embarrassment and discomfort. The girl was shivering. She was thirteen and he was slightly older. They were racing against time to give their folks what they had been anxiously anticipating. A white handkerchief smeared with the bride's fresh blood had to be delivered in order to trumpet the honor of the two families.

They had hardly known each other before that night. In fact, it was the groom's first time seeing his future wife, and there was no time to waste on kissing or foreplay. As if following a user's manual, he swiftly and mechanically did what he was supposed to do. The door was opened and a silky kerchief handed over to one of the ladies outside, to proclaim "mission accomplished." The women's ululations filled the air like fireworks. Their singing and clapping continued as they walked away to let the exhausted couple have some rest. Covered in sweat, the groom leaned on the door with a triumphant smile on his face. The bride was still lying in bed, crying in pain. After a while, they both fell into well-deserved deep sleep.

Eager to read my first adult book, I randomly picked the Egyptian novel from our home library, and I remember putting some very serious expressions on my face as I had seen my parents do while I flipped through its yellowish, crumbling pages. I neither remember the name of the novel nor the author now. Naturally, at my age then, I hadn't had the slightest idea where the blood on the handkerchief could have come from. The handkerchief tradition turned out to have been an ancient rural custom carried out by generations of Egyptians, Christians, and Muslims alike. Alas, things don't always go as planned and success was never guaranteed. That's why it was important to have a back-up plan.

In his novel *Al-Nabati*, which takes place in mid-seventh century, Youssef Zeidan—a prominent Egyptian author and scholar—illustrates a common solution to the problem. On his wedding night, Salameh and his sister Leila walk into the tent where his young bride Maria has been waiting in fear. Leila rests the bride's head on her lap and pulls her dress up so that her brother does what needs to be done. Maria hasn't told anyone that she'd lost her virginity to a stranger when she was a little girl. After several attempts, Leila suggests that her brother use his finger instead, but when he does, Maria feels an enormous pain inside and starts to cry. Leila softens up, tells him to step back, cuts her thigh, and puts a few drops of blood on the white kerchief. Salameh comes out of the tent to wave it at the tribe. And the celebration begins.

I tried unsuccessfully to track down the ritual's source online. Shakespeare mentioned something of the sort in *Othello*. There are also groups of gypsies in Europe who still to this day practice it on their weddings. I searched in the Koran, but couldn't find any reference to it there. Regardless of its origin, the scene as portrayed in the old Egyptian novel was my first encounter with this cultural oddity in which people shamelessly give themselves right to pry into other people's personal lives.

Scene Two

When I first set foot in Montreal, it was springtime. I went on a sightseeing tour and cruised on the St. Lawrence River. Everything seemed wonderful: great cuisine from all over the world, lots of festivals and concerts. And most importantly, people didn't seem to mind strangers—but I had the weird feeling something was missing. As I walked down into the Metro, I noticed people weren't looking at each other. There was no eye contact whatsoever. Every once in a while, I checked my reflection in the train window just to make sure I was still there. If not for the looks from tourists and little children, I would have thought I was invisible. For a moment there, I imagined people could walk through me.

I watched them come and go with their iPods—the iPad wasn't out yet—and disposable sipper cups. I couldn't understand why someone would sip coffee from a lidded paper cup and miss smelling its aroma. What's a cup of coffee without its seductive vapors? Turkish coffee had a distinctive air of elegance back in our house in Iraq. My mother made sure to let it brew at low heat and would serve it in small fine china cups with a thick layer of foam on top. Many people I knew loved to smoke while drinking their coffee. It was like meditation. But with Starbucks now flooding our Arab cities with endless choices of cappuccinos, mochachinos, frappuccinos, lattes, and espressos, it's really hard to get a cup of Turkish coffee as good as my mother's.

A pre-recorded female voice snapped me out of my coffee nostalgia to announce the next station. Some riders stepped off and others rushed in, all seeming unhappy and burdened. It may be natural for someone like me with a history of war and adversity to look sad. To my knowledge, there hadn't been a conflict in Quebec for ages. Why, then, did these people look so miserable? Actually, their frowns reminded me of the faces I had seen during a summer visit to Moscow with my family almost thirty years earlier.

The Soviet Union was at its peak then, and from my hotel room I watched people lining up in front of a small cabin that sold ice-cream bars, all of which were the same product, the same size, and the same flavor. The lifeless faces of the Russians waiting for ice cream resembled those of the Montrealers in the Metro, despite this occasion's abundance of choice and flavor. For many years I had thought life in a less intrusive culture than ours should be much easier. But there I was in Montreal, a city whose inhabitants have the utmost respect for human privacy, almost devoid of judgments and prejudice. And yet, the people there were still not happy.

Scene Three

Privacy has no actual meaning in Arab culture. We spy on each other all the time. Family, friends, and neighbors scrutinize and analyze your every gesture. Our minds are programmed to weave threads of scandal and conspiracy, and we have trained our senses to help us there too. Our eyes peek, our noses sniff, and our ears eavesdrop. One gets used to playing the surveillance game over time. Mind you, it's actually fun, but you have to be careful because the game can turn against the player at any given moment. Everyone is subject to all types of accusations. And unless they prove themselves innocent, they will be in big trouble.

When the phone rang late that night, I knew something bad must have happened. "The Haji has been shot," said the quivering voice on the other end of the line. My family had a small commercial building on Palestine Street and the Haji—a title given to a man who has performed the pilgrimage to Mecca—was renting one of its apartments as a business bureau. Almost a month before this call, I had received an alarming call from one of the Haji's neighbors in the building: "You have to do something about it. Every night we see young girls go inside his apartment, and then we hear them laugh and moan loud. We tried to warn him, but he refused to listen. This is shameful and disgusting."

When I confronted him with his neighbors' grievances, the Haji rebuffed everything and assured me that all allegations were false. "I'm an honorable, religious married man," he said solemnly, and then went on lecturing me on moral decency, not forgetting to remind me of his Mecca trip. The police arrested the shooter after a couple of weeks: he turned out to be one of the girls' brothers. A neighbor was able to recognize the girl while she stood at the Haji's door, and he told her family. The Haji miraculously survived the shooting and agreed to leave the apartment after he was released from the hospital. He rented another love nest in another neighborhood, I was told.

Many men keep secret wives or mistresses, or they just like to have sex with prostitutes. The Haji was definitely not the only playboy in town. "He should have known better," a friend said when I told him about the incident. "I know a businessman who rented a small house to meet his married mistress, but the neighbors would not leave them in peace. They knocked on the door and demanded to know who the woman was and why she was visiting him in his place. He was quite shrewd. He invited them for tea and introduced them to her, claiming that she was a married sister and she'd only come to look after him." The story was convincing, especially because the mistress was keen to arrive and leave wearing *hijab*. She even became friends with the women of the neighborhood who admired her dedication to serving her lonely brother.

Scene Four

I was on my way to fetch my father from his clinic one night when I saw her. I thought her face looked familiar. I had seen the lady in the Islamic dress who crossed the street in front of my car, but I couldn't remember where or when until I reached my father's clinic: *Of course, she's Samira!* I surmised that she was heading to the nearby theater where she played, sang, and danced in costumes which showed much more of her body than did the conservative dress she was wearing when I saw her. I had seen her several times on television, but she wasn't covering then.

A friend of mine who claimed to know Samira told me that when the play was over, she spent the rest of the night "escorting" rich admirers. "Unlike what most people think, acting is not a well-paying career in Iraq, and she has a large family to feed," he elaborated. "Her neighbors don't mind her reputation as long as she does her things away from them. She's a very kind-hearted person." Samira gave the neighbors what they wanted so that they'd let her feed her family. She, like many of us, wore a disguise to elude the vigilant snipers.

Scene Five

I doubt there could be a compliment more gratifying than being told, "You are as generous as Hatem Al-Ta'ie." The prolific sixth-century poet died shortly after the Prophet's birth. Some sources say he was a Christian; others insist that he followed a monotheistic faith that was neither Judaism nor Christianity. Either way, Hatem had surely outlived his time to become an icon of Arab generosity. Tradition has it that when a stranger arrived at his door late one night, he invited him inside and secretly ordered his precious and only horse to be slain and cooked. When the guest woke up the next day, he noticed the absence of his host's horse and realized his great sacrifice. Al-Ta'ie was henceforth deemed the most generous person of all.

I remember well the dramatic voice of our teacher in class wrapping up the story: "And indeed he was." To be honest, I wasn't convinced then, and I'm still not convinced that what Hatem Al-Ta'ie had done was out of sheer generosity. It would have been fairly generous of him had he offered the stranger whatever food he and his family were surviving on. Some milk, dates, and a piece of bread would have perfectly sufficed. But not for a man with Hatem's pride. He was willing to do anything and everything to maintain a towering stature among the other tribes. More than fourteen centuries have passed since the night Al-Ta'ie killed his horse to feed a stranger guest, and yet little has changed.

We still make enormous efforts—often beyond our abilities and resources—to impress other people. We fight tooth and nail over who pays the bill at restaurants or coffee shops. The fight could take a good long while, but it doesn't really matter, for the prize is extremely rewarding. Our obsession with keeping a polished public image shows in our houses as well. Most domiciles have a guest room and a living room, the former being for visitors and the latter, for family members. There is a bathroom for guests and another, or others, for the family. Guest spaces should always be spotless, tidy, and fragrant because they represent the side of us we would like strangers to see. The family zone on the other hand, with some exceptions, only gets minimal attention. Strangers don't see it.

During the hard years of the nineties, a whole generation of Iraqi children grew up in deprivation. Some parents joked that their children panicked when they saw a banana for the first time. Those who were fortunate enough to have relatives living abroad occasionally received gifts of fruits, chocolates, and cola. Some of them would carefully place the empty boxes, tins, and peels next to their doors to let the neighbors know how privileged they were.

Scene Six

Ashamed and defeated, I walked into my room, locked the door, and cried like a little boy. It was one of difficult decisions—if not the most difficult—I'd ever made, but I had no other choice. My only aunt has Alzheimer's disease, and she has no children. I had been looking after her since she came to live with us in Jordan, but it was time for us to leave. I couldn't send her back to Baghdad because it was total chaos there. And I couldn't take her with me either. I knew she would get proper medical care in the rest home I'd found, and she probably wouldn't miss me. By that time, she could hardly recognize who I was. But what would people say? Even though I hadn't done anything wrong, the question weighed heavily on my mind.

Five years later, the bitterness has lessened a bit. I've been visiting my aunt twice a year, and she seems to be doing well, but I still haven't stopped worrying about what people think of me for putting her there, and doubt that I ever will. It may be acceptable in other cultures, but it's absolutely abhorrent for Arab men to put their parents in nursing homes. It's also unacceptable for sons—impossible for daughters—to leave their parents' houses before marrying. There are always lines to beware of crossing, or shame will befall us.

Customs and traditions are not all bad, really. The Arab elderly, for instance, or most of them, don't suffer from loneliness like their counterparts in the West do. They live with their families and are looked after and amused by their children and grandchildren, who, on the other hand, grow up relishing the love and attention of both their parents and their grandparents. In many Arab cities and villages, it's not uncommon to find three or four generations of the same family living together in one dwelling.

I had a friend in school that lived with his parents, brothers, aunts, uncles, cousins, and grandparents in one big house. I remember telling him once that their house looked like Noah's Ark. He said our house was as quiet as a library or a hospital. Deep inside, I envied him. There was always something interesting going on at their home, and it seemed like a lot of fun to live there. But I guess the grass is always greener on the other side. My friend frequently complained about the noise and lack of privacy in his home.

In an environment as harsh as the Arabian Desert, it was impossible for individuals to survive without clustering together in tribes. Their togetherness empowered them and protected them from the many dangers that lurked outside. But along with protection came the restriction of personal freedoms, and obedience to rules and authority. The deserts now are much safer than they used to be. Modern cities with gleaming skyscrapers have been built, and we no longer live in tents or ride camels and horses. Our nomadic forebears' feelings of insecurity still inhabit our collective psyche, nevertheless. And we still have to abide by their old precepts, good and bad.

Scene Seven

While Jews pride themselves on being God's chosen people, Christians believe they are saved by Jesus, who laid down his life for them. The verse I've put at the beginning gives us Muslims a very good reason to be proud too. Not only are we the best among all the other nations, as God Himself tells us, but we are also on a holy mission to rectify this world. The designation is undeniably ego-boosting, but things are not as clear-cut as they were many centuries ago. Righteousness is not so obvious; nor is evil. They both have been camouflaged.

During the time of idolatry, the brothels of Mecca raised red flags to distinguish themselves from their surroundings. When Islam prohibited the business, they were all shut down immediately. Today's prostitution is largely versatile: physical, audio-visual, and in many cases virtual. Instead of idols made of stone or wood, people worship living idols: actors, singers, athletes, and reality-TV stars. The old-time usurers have given way to bankers and businessmen. They may not be allowed to confiscate and sell our sons and daughters if we fail to pay our debts on time, but their gigantic corporations still control our lives, pushing many of us to the verge of despair, even suicide.

Just as the Arabian tribes attacked and pillaged one another in the old times, today's strong nations oppress the weak. In the name of justice and human rights they send their armies to invade them, steal from them, and incite civil wars and bloodshed. I'm not dramatizing. Our world is not in any way less errant than it had been when God sent Mohammed to lead mankind onto the right path. It's only *differently* errant. But there will be no other prophet after Mohammed; God has made it clear in the Koran. Jesus was the Messiah promised to the Jews, and now that he has ascended to heaven, there isn't going to be a successor. It is every Muslim's duty to correct wrong whenever and wherever it might be, with our hands, our tongues, and our hearts, the Prophet decreed in one of his famous sayings.

This undertaking is both challenging and dangerous in the fogginess of our modern times. Is it beneficent to force women to cover and non-Muslims to convert to Islam? Is it malevolent to listen to music and enjoy art and literature? If we were to ask a fanatic Muslim and a liberal Muslim, we would receive contradictory answers. They are both Muslims, nonetheless, and are hence prescribed and encouraged to rectify. But we cannot possibly "enjoin beneficence and forbid malevolence" unless we define which is which first. Which is *marouf* (beneficent) and which is *munkar* (malevolent)? I'm afraid there's no other means to do so than by imposing scrutiny and passing judgment. We judge each other's looks, acts, ideas, and opinions. Although in contrast with the Koranic commands to refrain from judging, we actually judge everyone and everything.

CHAPTER 4

"You Are Divorced!"

AND THEIR LORD ANSWERED THEIR PRAYER: I
WASTE NOT THE DEEDS OF ANY OF YOU, MALE
OR FEMALE, MEMBERS ONE OF ANOTHER.

(3.195)

I'm often irritated by the widely circulated stereotype of Arab women because I know it's not true. Well, at least it's not true in my mother's case, or the cases of so many women I've known. Not even once in my life have I felt that she was inferior to my father or blindly obedient to him. As a matter of fact, she was and still is quite the opposite of that, an independent equal partner. Oh, and need I say that she didn't cover her hair either? Strangely enough, back when I was a child in Baghdad, no one seemed to mind it, nor did anyone consider her less of a Muslim because of it.

But my mother wasn't the only one. Most of my schoolmates had uncovered, working moms. Also, neither of our fathers had other wives than our mothers; although it wouldn't have been against the law or religion to have had them, polygamy was socially frowned upon.

At that time, Baghdadi society was influenced by Western culture and Western ideals. The Iraqi alumni of

European and American universities were returning home, implementing new social trends and making the period of time between the fifties and the eighties of the last century the glory days of modern Iraqi feminism.

Scene One

A few years had passed since war had broken out between Iraq and Iran in 1980. People had already adapted to living with Iranian air raids and started to reinvigorate their social lives. Fierce battles took place every now and then on the frontlines, quite far from the capital. My parents were having distant relatives, a couple with three little girls, over for dinner. After dinner the ladies retired to our living room to chat. I happened to be sitting there, enjoying my exquisite meal while watching something interesting on television. It didn't take me long to realize the unfolding story behind my back was more tempting than whatever drama I was watching.

The pretty young wife confided to my mother that her husband was thinking about taking another wife. They had three daughters already, but he wanted a boy to carry on the family name, a desire shared by most Arab husbands and many non-Arabs as well. I was just stepping into my teens, inexperienced with relationships. I remember feeling sorry for her because she was obviously in emotional agony. She helplessly succumbed to her husband's desire, and whispering her bitterness was all she could do about it. No rage, no yelling, no packing up and slamming the door? Her reaction seemed weird to me. I couldn't help wondering whether my father too might decide to marry another wife. What if one day he wanted to start a new family and have more children? What would my friends say? Thankfully, that never happened, but just thinking about the possibility was outrageous for the boy I was then.

Sharing a spouse with another woman would be a mortifying reflection for any Muslim wife to consider, much less experience. Had something like that happened to my mother, for example, I haven't the slightest doubt that she would have filed for divorce immediately. Her pride couldn't have swallowed the insult. But my mother was working, and she could have relied on her own resources to survive. I felt more sympathy towards women like our poor guest who was totally dependent on her husband both financially and socially. It was my first face-to-face encounter with polygamy, and I found it revolting. But as I've mentioned earlier, the eighties marked a significant deterioration of women's rights not only in Iraq, but in many Arab and Islamic countries as well. Iran's Islamic Revolution, the Soviet invasion of Afghanistan, and the rise of Islamic extremism all contributed to halting the ambitious movement of Arab and Islamic feminism.

During the war with Iran, Saddam was willing to do anything to insure his army's loyalty. He showered them with privileges, and they ended up dominating the social scene in the country, inflicting their values on the rest of the community. The role of academics was marginalized. They were no longer the role models or trendsetters they used to be. The eight-year conflict killed and disabled hundreds of thousands of young men on both sides, and it was only natural that the officers and soldiers who returned home for a short period of time would try to live life to the fullest. To hell with the Western values and ideals of the educated middle class. For them, it was life versus death.

Not knowing whether they'd live to see the next leave, they unleashed their every curbed desire, and sex always came on top of their bucket lists.

Also, in light of the increasing number of spinsters and widows among Iraqi women, and the enormous losses of men during the war, polygamy did make some sense at the time: it provided solutions, if not necessarily fair ones, and was becoming more and more accepted. Justified by religion, Muslim polygamists claimed to have been following the Prophet's example. Stories of second, third, and fourth wives began circulating. Even the president had secretly taken a second wife.

Prophet Mohammed didn't come up with polygamy; he didn't invent it. Abraham, David, and Solomon had all taken more than one wife. In Arabia, polygamy had been practiced without limitations for centuries before the Prophet was even born. As a matter of fact, Islam restricted it to four wives, requiring the husband to treat each with fairness and equality. Which is practically impossible.

One of the first things I failed to comprehend as a child was the paradox of the Prophet's several marriages. Despite leading a life of renunciation, Mohammed kept marrying more and more women. His first wife, a widow he loved dearly, was fifteen years his senior. She was his only wife for the twenty-five years of their marriage, and it was only after her death that he would marry another woman, and then another, and another.

At school we were taught that the Prophet married his numerous wives (as many as eleven, although that number is disputed) for social and political reasons. I have no idea who first drew that ridiculous conclusion, but I know it's still popular and widely accepted by many Muslims. In one of his famous sayings, the Prophet admitted that of all the pleasures in life, he enjoyed perfume and women the most, even though he found the most comfort and peace of mind in prayer. I must say here that I have only managed to understand and value Mohammed's humanness fairly recently.

Scene Two

As I grew into puberty, I was able to better comprehend what motivates men to have affairs. I understood how strong, almost uncontainable, a man's sex drive can be. And while the issue of men being polygamous and women monogamous by nature is debatable, supported by some sexologists and denied by others, I honestly doubt there exists a man who hadn't harbored the fantasy of it at one point or another in his life. I'm not proud to admit it, but the thought crossed my mind too when I was an adolescent, and not infrequently.

In a perfect world, love, sex, and marriage should go together, but that may not be the case in our deeply imperfect world! In my opinion, love is one thing but marriage is another. All the same, sex is an important part of marriage, and except for platonic stories, sex is strongly associated with love too. That said, sexual practice can be made on its own merit, an animalistic impulse without emotional attachment or social commitment. Although doomed and forbidden by almost all religions, it's been happening since life began and will continue for as long as humans exist.

What if a married man or woman were to fall in love with someone other than his or her spouse? During my search for definitions of love, sex, and marriage, I had to ask this question. Since falling in love is like catching a virus, something beyond our control, it can happen at any given minute. We can always try to resist it, of course, but let's face it, not all of us have good immunity against love and sexual desire.

These days, more and more couples choose to live together instead of marrying. Out-of-wedlock births are climbing to an all-time high in the West, and likewise the retreat from marriage. Thousands of children are born to teenage mothers who have absolutely no means to support themselves or their children. The governments pay for the care of the mother and her child, but children may never get to meet or even know whom their fathers are.

According to Islamic scholars, in order to avoid this very dilemma, polygamy was legalized. It gave children the right to know and bear their fathers' names, and it placed legal obligation upon fathers to honor their social and financial responsibilities towards their sons, daughters, and wives. Polygamy, these scholars stress, has proved to be effective in times of war, providing opportunities for widowed wives and orphaned children to enjoy normal, or almost normal, family life again. It has saved many women from spinster-hood as well.

While polygamy has been a solution to several social

predicaments, it has created others. Children may bear their fathers' names, but they rarely have the chance to spend time with them, much less enjoy their love and attention. This lack of communication between father and son can result in serious psychological disorders, quite similar to those suffered by Western children who miss having a father figure in their lives. Islamic polygamy also raises ethical questions—at least on my part—about the validity of solving a woman's problem, or even a man's, at the cost of another human being's happiness and dignity.

I once talked to an observant Muslim woman whose husband was having an affair. A friend had seen him with a blonde woman in a restaurant. The distressed wife was crying her eyes out when I came home and heard her telling my parents her agonizing story. I suggested that she confront him and make him choose between her and the other woman, but she refused. She was afraid he might choose the blonde over her. Knowing how religious she was, I thought she was devastated because she couldn't stand the thought of being married to a sinful man, an adulterer. Stupidly and without giving much thought, I suggested that she let him marry the other woman. With a look of sheer panic, she cried, "I beg of you, for God's sake, don't ever mention that in front of him!" I never again brought up the subject, but I realized in that moment that no woman, no matter how religious she may be, could withstand the insult of her husband taking another wife. In the end, she let him continue his secret affair with the blonde woman, whom he never married anyway.

Scene Three

Polygamy is not the only complexity Muslim women face in their everyday lives. Actually, there is a long list of things to worry about or accept as unchangeable facts: the lack of recognition, the deprivation of the right to an education, the ban on mobility unless in the company of a male relative. But these restrictions vary widely from one Islamic country to another. While Saudi women can barely reveal their faces and hands in public, Muslim women in Turkey or Lebanon can openly sunbathe on the beach in nothing but a bikini. Men and women are strictly separated in extremely conservative societies. In hospitals and universities as well as on public transportation, no mixing between the sexes is allowed. Women's voices, with the exception of low tones and whispers, are not to be heard in the presence of men they do not know. And men in turn avoid mentioning their female relatives in their conversations.

When I was in the army, an officer summoned me one day and told me that my sister, a physician, had treated his wife. The funny part was when his words didn't seem to make much sense to me. *Sister* and *wife*, according to his tribal traditions, were bad, more like swear words! "Your *female-breast-milk-sibling* saw my *harem*, and she told me about you." I remember it took me lots of *what*s and *who*s before I realized he was talking about my sister and his wife. It was the silliest thing I'd ever heard, and I still don't get how such a stupid, totally unnecessary twisting of words could be more decent than saying it plainly and simply. The sentence was also quite inaccurate because my mother, due to some health issues, had hardly breastfed me after I was born!

Scene Four

The application of personal status laws in different Islamic countries and their claimed derivation of Sharia law is yet another controversy. In Tunisia, for instance, gender equality is guaranteed in the constitution. Of course, with all the emerging political changes in the country, there is the potential to amend the constitution to deprive Tunisian women of their privileges, including the right to give their family names to their children of unknown fathers. Domestic violence is still punished there; polygamy is illegal; and since 1981, the Tunisian government has imposed a ban on head-covering in the public realm, which I think is quite coercive. Although not a supporter of covering, I believe everyone should be free to dress the way they choose.

Secular Tunisia and Turkey are both members of the Organization of Islamic Cooperation, just like Afghanistan, Iran, and Saudi Arabia, where different types of law—obviously anti-feminist—regulate people's lives. The Iraqi Personal Status Law is middle-of-the-road, not as liberal as the Tunisian or the Turkish, but not bigoted either. Iraqi women are eligible to sign their own marriage contracts if they so wish, a very basic right denied to women in several Islamic countries, where a marriage contract signed by the bride could easily be voided. Whether the bride is eigh-teen years old or fifty, and whether she's illiterate or has a doctoral degree in astronomy, her male guardian's consent and presence remain crucial in validating her marriage contract, even if that male guardian—usually the father or brother or uncle—happens to be a criminal or a drug addict.

Among Muslim men's many privileges over women, we have the right to divorce our wives easily and arbitrarily. All that is necessary for a man to put an end to his marriage is uttering the following phrase to his wife: "You are divorced!" The wife will then have to fight a long court battle to get a modest alimony for herself and her children. Muslim husbands can threaten their wives with divorce for any given reason, no matter how trivial: "If you don't bring me a glass of cold water now, you will be divorced!" The wife, who might be exhausted or sick, has to bring her husband the glass of cold water or else she will literally have to risk being divorced. They will have to remarry if they want to resume living together.

Some Muslim men abuse the privileges granted to them. For instance, when a Bedouin man invites someone for dinner, out of warm hospitality, he could say, "If you won't come to dine with me tonight, my wife will be divorced!" If the guest, for whatever reason, doesn't show up, the wife—who may have been working like a dog all day to please her husband and his friends—will indeed be considered divorced. Yes, it's as simple and unfair as that, and it can hit any Muslim wife and turn her life upside down at any moment. I'm not against divorce, myself. It should be left to a married couple to decide whether they wish to stay together or go their separate ways. However, coercion is or should be out of the question.

Prenuptial agreements are becoming increasingly popular in the West. We often hear about celebrity couples signing them before tying the knot. Muslim women, I only recently found out, have long been entitled to list all their expectations of partnership in their marriage contracts. Once a prospective husband agrees to his prospective wife's conditions, they become compulsory under law. Among those conditions, a Muslim woman can insist that her husband never take another wife, and she may also claim the right to obtain a divorce when and if she wants it. This all sounds great in theory, but in reality, only a few women assert their legal rights. Most women are not allowed to read their marriage contracts, let alone sign them. They don't even know such rights exist. In our traditionally patriarchal societies, the majority of women choose to conform to social standards, rather than challenge them. Women who dare stand up for their rights are looked upon as disgraceful. They bring shame on their families.

Scene Five

Embarrassed and not knowing how to approach the vendor inside, I walked back and forth in front of the silverware shop. It was my first time selling something, anything. I had a set of six sterling-silver napkin rings in a wrinkled green plastic bag that had the name Harrods printed on it. My mother must have kept that bag from our last visit to London more than ten years earlier. The memory of that trip had long faded away. We'd gone through two wars since then. Unlike the war with Iran, the war in 1991 was short but a lot more destructive.

Those years were so hard on us. Many Iraqis had to sell family heirlooms and personal belongings to survive. During the twelve years of global sanctions that only ended after the ousting of Saddam in 2003 by yet another destructive war, the Iraqi dinar's value went down the drain. Once worth more than three American dollars, the dinar plunged to less than a tenth of a cent. Our life savings became worthless, and people started dying of hunger and illness.

I finally dragged myself into the shop and sold the napkin rings that had beautiful illustrations of Iraqi ruins hand-drawn around the middle of each ring in black enamel. I hurriedly left with the sum of one hundred American dollars in my pocket to buy a new pair of tires for my car. It was a rainy winter, and the roads were becoming dangerously slippery. Looking back now, I think we were fortunate to have made it through those tough years. Many Iraqis didn't.

I will never forget the sad story of two destitute sisters who lived in the slums of Baghdad. Their mother died when they were young, and their father was later killed in one of the wars. The girls struggled night and day to earn a living, but they were sexually harassed in every workplace and at every turn; when they resisted, they were badly insulted and thrown out onto the street. One night, they sat down to talk about their future and came up with a horrible idea. They poured the little kerosene left in their rusty heater on themselves and set themselves on fire. The sisters died embracing each other, and it was impossible to separate their burnt corpses the next day. In a country that had the second-largest reserves of crude oil in the world, two starving girls used oil to put an end to their unbearable lives.

They were crushingly poor, but they could never sell their bodies for money, no matter how tempting the offers they received. Their parents had taught them to honor and protect their bodies, so they decided to kill themselves rather than allow strangers to desecrate them. Other girls, especially those who were responsible for feeding their families with no resources other than their flesh, had no other choice but to turn to prostitution. They slept with whoever could afford to pay their modest prices. The prettier girls sought more profitable markets abroad to sell their merchandise. Iraqi prostitutes flooded the streets of Jordan, the only country still allowing Iraqis in during the nineties. Saddam, who had tactically turned religious at the time, issued new regulations that banned women from traveling alone. No Iraqi female could leave the country without an escorting father, brother, or husband. This ban continued until 2003, depriving many girls—including those who had no intention of becoming prostitutes—of the right to work and study outside the country.

Iraqi women had been traveling freely since the early twentieth century. Many had pursued their postgraduate studies in Lebanon, Europe, and the United States. Saddam's ban was by all means a slap in the face of feminism. It wasn't the only one, though. But instead of pinpointing the actual causes of prostitution and questioning the dictator about oppressing and starving his people and the several futile wars he had waged, a further reduction on the already-small margin of freedoms given to women came about. Once again, it was women who had to pay the price.

Scene Six

When I was a child, I remember hearing my parents talk about a husband who had come back home unexpectedly early one day and seen his wife having sex with a stranger in their bed. Blinded by fury, he pulled out his pistol and shot them both dead. The judge sentenced him to only seven years imprisonment, considering the state of shock he must have been in when committing the murders. Had the wife been put in that terrible position, had she been the one who'd pulled the trigger, I'm certain the judge would have shown very little sympathy.

In the Koran, God says adulterers, men or women, should receive equal punishment. The courts in several Islamic countries, however, think and act otherwise. Judges often give reduced sentences to men convicted of murdering female members of their families over *suspicions* of adultery. They call it honor killing. I have found horrible stories online about Muslim men who slaughtered their wives, daughters, sisters, nieces, or cousins. They got away with their crimes, respected and admired in their communities even when their suspicions were later refuted by autopsy reports that determined many of the slain girls were in fact virgins.

Having lived in the city my entire life, I knew very little about those crimes, which were more common in rural areas. Therefore I was appalled when I watched an online video of a girl being publicly stoned to death by an angry mob. I tried to find more information about the crime. Du'a Khalil Aswad was a seventeen-year-old Yazidi from the town of Bashika in northern Iraq. Some sources said that she had converted to Islam and run away with her Muslim boyfriend; others insisted that they'd only been seen talking together. I was in New Zealand when I saw Du'a bleeding in Bashika's town square, her body rising and falling while people kicked her and threw stones at her. It was 2008 and I had left Iraq two years earlier. I remember feeling deeply ashamed. Du'a too was found a virgin.

Scene Seven

Yes, many of the barriers to gender equity in Muslim communities are man-made. Our male-biased traditions may appear to have religious grounds, but most of them are products of long centuries of dominant masculinity; they have nothing to do with religion. Islamic laws are not totally bias-free, either. The inheritance law, to give one example, entitles brothers to receive twice the inheritance of their sisters.

Islamic scholars say all Muslim men are legally obligated to provide for their wives, children, mothers, and sisters. A woman's share of any inheritance is hers alone; she may spend it any way she desires. Justifications like these may sound convincing, but on the ground, it's a different story. I personally know several Muslim men who—despite having inherited twice as much as their sisters—spend hardly any money on maintaining their needy female relatives. Why not give women their full share instead of making them beg for it?

I've also had a hard time grasping why a woman's testimony in court is only worth half that of a man's. Muslim clerics say women are naturally emotional: they undergo hormonal changes that influence their behavior and thereby the credibility of their legal testimony. But what about our male hormones? Have not male lusts and arrogance done enough damage to the world already? In the Koran, God says two women witnesses are needed so that if one of them forgets certain details or makes mistakes, the other could correct her. But shouldn't that apply to male witnesses as well? Don't men forget and make mistakes too?

In Iraq, women have occupied many leading positions. There are women doctors, professors, engineers, lawyers, judges, parliament members, and ministers, whereas in a few other Islamic countries, women have become prime ministers and heads of state. My point is that if women are eligible for such key positions; if their raging hormones and emotions didn't keep them from meeting the difficult requirements of their jobs; if they can be relied upon to teach students, cure patients, defend clients, and issue verdicts in court; and if women can be entrusted with the welfare and future planning of their nations, then why can't they be trusted to testify in court?

If Zaha Hadid—the world-renowned, Iraqi-born British architect and first woman recipient of the prestigious Pritzker Prize (known as the architects' Nobel)—were ever to consider returning to her birthplace one day, her legal testimony would only carry half the weight of that of an illiterate eighteen-year-old boy. Sadly then, neither Hadid's world reputation nor her prestigious Pritzker could do a thing to change that.

Scene Eight

The status of Muslim women represents an accurate barometer of their nation's progress over the centuries. As opposed to the infamous harems of the Ottoman sultans, there have been many innovative female role models, starting with Aisha, the Prophet's beloved and last wife, a leading figure acknowledged by Muslim men and women alike. After Mohammed's death, she dedicated her life to explaining his teachings to the growing masses of believers. In the eighth century, Rabi'a Al Adawiyya, a woman mystic and ascetic, set forth the creed of Divine Love. Adawiyya has thousands of followers and admirers around the world to this day. Another powerful Muslim woman was Shajarat Al Durr, who ruled Egypt in the thirteenth century and proved to have impressive courage and might.

God narrates the stories of several women throughout the scriptures: Adam's wife (unlike the Bible, the Koran does not mention her name); Moses' mother, sister, and foster-mother; the Virgin Mary; the queen of Sheba; the wives of Noah, Abraham, Lot, Job, and Zacharias. There is hardly a page in the Koran that doesn't mention or instruct women. In addition to the chapter Al-Nisa'a (The Women), there are numerous Koranic verses that discuss womanly issues like puberty, menstruation, menopause, personal hygiene, dress code, marriage, dowry, divorce, alimony, sex, pregnancy, praying, almsgiving, and pilgrimage. Hundreds, if not thousands, of the Prophet's sayings revolve around women. In a famous saying, the Prophet compared women to glass vessels, and as such, he instructed Muslim men to handle them with extreme care and gentleness.

Many women today, especially in the West, would argue against and may even resent the comparison with thin glass. Women, they'd likely say, are as strong and independent as men, and if anything only need men to treat them as equals. I have no doubt of the benign intentions behind the Prophet's comparison; indeed, I'm often impressed by the courage and resolution of women. Iraqi women in particular have been incredibly persistent in challenging and surmounting the countless obstacles put in their way. They have taken charge and struggled to raise, protect, and educate their children under the most difficult circumstances inside and outside of Iraq. Those brave women have shown a will of steel that not the strongest men, nor even mighty wars, were able to defeat. I have absolutely no shame in saying that I look up to them.

CHAPTER 5

On Being Different

AND WHEN LOT SAID TO HIS PEOPLE: DO YOU
COMMIT LEWDNESS THAT NO OTHER CREA-
TURE HAS COMMITTED BEFORE YOU? YOU
APPROACH MEN IN LUST INSTEAD OF WOMEN.
YOU ARE INDEED A WANTON PEOPLE.

(7.80,81)

Ever since I was a child in Iraq, I've had nagging questions in my head that needed to be answered or at least
asked. I thought someday, when I was old enough, I might
write an article or even a book about them. It never crossed
my mind though that I'd end up writing about sexuality,
much less homosexuality!

Despite our reputation as being extremely sensual, sex
is a topic we Arabs don't feel comfortable discussing in
public, and to be honest, it wasn't until I had met my childhood friend Hassan a few years ago in Jordan that I realized
homosexuality, and the way we dealt with it, was actually at
the core of this book's premise. I decided to challenge my
cultural constraints and write a page or two about it. But as
I started writing, I found out I had much more to say.

Scene One

"If I happened to find Aladdin's magic lamp one day, and the genie allowed me three wishes, my first would be: *Turn me into a heterosexual!*"

Those were the last words I expected to hear from Rami, a young gay man and a friend of a friend of mine. Given the sensitivity of the topic, I thought he might refuse to talk about it, but surprisingly, he didn't mind; the three of us— Rami, our mutual friend, and I—sat around a small table in a coffee shop, conversing. Rami was studying medicine and had just come back from a short visit to Saudi Arabia, where his father was working. It was my first time meeting Rami, and he seemed tense and uncomfortable divulging his most intimate secrets to a stranger, which I totally understood.

"Why are you writing about homosexuality?" he asked me almost immediately after we shook hands. Another question I did not expect!

"Well, because it obviously exists." I couldn't think of a better answer.

He went on grilling me: "And what will you say about it, that it's not *haram* (sinful and forbidden)? I'm sure you know that sodomy is one of the things that repulses Allah the most. Haven't you read the story of Lot in the Koran?"

At that point, without knowing it, Rami sounded like one of the puritanical Muslims who'd been targeting, humiliating, and in some cases, murdering homosexuals like himself. I tried to explain to him that it was never my intention to issue judgments, nor to declare what's sinful and what's not. My only concern, I stressed, was to discuss the way our Arab-Muslim community dealt with homosexuality.

Our meeting coincided with the news about sexual cleansing in Iraq. Militiamen, based on a religious decree, had been chasing gays down the streets of Baghdad and other Iraqi cities. They tortured them in a most barbaric way: they glued their anuses shut with strong adhesives, and to further add to the torment, fed them powerful laxatives until they died of blocked or ruptured bowels.

"Let me ask you this question, Ali," Rami said. "If you had a gay son, how would you feel if he invited his partner to your house one day, and you caught them having sex in his room?"

Rami's question made me reflect on the possibility and triggered additional questions in my head about it. How would I respond if I were put in that situation? Would I see red and throw them both out of the house? Would I batter or even kill my gay son like some fathers had done in similar situations? Of course, I would hope I'd be able to absorb the shock, control my anger, and quietly talk things over with him. But what would be there to talk about?

My mind scattered in multiple directions, weighing the pros and cons of possible solutions. Perhaps it would be best to send him to live abroad, sparing him and myself all the turmoil? Or maybe I should ask him to hide it and pretend to be what he is not? My confusion must have shown clearly. There was a triumphant smile on Rami's face. His hypothetical question had caught me off guard, and it was such a relief to remember that I neither had a gay son nor was married in the first place!

He then told me about his boomerang relationship with a high-school mate. They fought all the time, broke up, and made up again. Rami wasn't happy with it, and he was also hurt when people mocked him for his sexuality, either at the university or in his neighborhood. He hoped his family would never figure it out, which I thought unrealistic because his feminine demeanor was too obvious to be ignored. I reckon his family, like many others, had chosen to live in denial. He had been rescued from suicide two or three times, as well. His parents blamed it on the stress of studying and exams, but he said he still sometimes thought of trying again.

"A gay friend of mine had a devious plan to avoid confrontation with his religious family," Rami said. "They kept pressuring him to marry his cousin, so he decided to marry the girl for a short time, have a child or two, and give everyone the proof of 'straightness' they sought. Then he'd divorce his wife, give the children to his parents to raise, and enjoy a relatively pressure-free homosexual life parallel to his feigned straight one as a divorced man."

In that dreadful scenario, Rami's friend would sacrifice the lives and future of several innocent people—his prospective wife and children—in order to save his reputation. He would be using them as human shields! I recollected the horrible incineration of hundreds of Iraqi civilians who'd gathered inside Al Amiriya bunker in Baghdad one night during the Gulf War in 1991. They didn't know the shelter was being secretly used as a military command unit at the time, or so claimed the United States after its stealth bombers dropped laser-guided bombs on the heavily reinforced concrete sanctuary, burning everyone there to ashes. Rami's friend's plan would not involve bombs and fire, but it still had the potential to destroy lives.

I thanked Rami for his time, we shook hands again, and then he walked out of the coffee shop. His eyes seemed lifeless despite the faint smile on his lips. Our mutual friend later told me that Rami got upset each time he saw a happily married couple hanging out with their children. The sight of them reminded him of a life he longed for but might never be able to have. I was sorry to hear that, but I think it embodies the dilemma of many homosexuals in our community.

We instinctively feel apprehensive towards those who are different from ourselves. We consider them a potential threat to our security; their mere existence in our lives freaks us out. I know because I've experienced it firsthand. During and after the last war in 2003, my life was a nightmare: I was losing the people I loved one after the other. Insanity prevailed, forcing me to withdraw into solitude. I lost faith and stopped praying. I also questioned the purpose of getting married and having children while people were dying in vain every day. Why should I become attached to people only to suffer their loss or leave them suffering mine? Had I not had a fair share of suffering already? I was physically and mentally drained, and all I wanted from life was to be left alone. I secluded myself from everyone and started writing, which became my only solace. It was a personal choice, and it wasn't going to affect anyone else's life but mine. However, and to my big surprise, it drove all the people I knew crazy.

First, they tried to persuade me to change my mind. I was touched. I thought it was kind of them to put effort and time into convincing a friend to make what they thought were the right decisions in life. But then they started attacking me. They said I might end up being sick or paralyzed with no one to look after me. I'd die alone and my body would rot before someone would notice my absence, and there would be no one to carry me to my grave anyway! I'd spend all my savings and then start begging when I could not work anymore. No one would care to read my book, either… if I were even fortunate enough to get published in the first place.

I kept telling them I was not against marriage. And by declining it, I knew I might live to regret it someday. But after all I'd been through, I felt I had nothing left to share, nothing that could give steady and lasting happiness to another human being. And the last thing I wanted to do was to make the people I loved, or would love, miserable.

Like starving jackals devouring their prey, my friends had a frightening sadistic gleam in their eyes while they argued with me. I began to put two and two together. It wasn't actually about me. They were using me as an excuse to give free rein to their own anger and frustration. They hated their jobs, and despite having friends and children, they often complained that their lives seemed empty... but they still insisted I be like them, nonetheless!

In the least rude way possible, I asked my friends to shut up and mind their own business. I have to admit, that experience showed me how people can be petrified by change and difference even when they are not personally affected. It was a turning point in the way I observed conversion, homosexuality, and the persecution of religious or ethnic minorities in any society. I guess that was one of the many things in my life I got to learn the hard way.

Scene Two

The Koran mentions the story of Lot in several chapters. In fact, all three Abrahamic traditions refer to the sinful people of Sodom and Gomorrah, and they all portray God's wrath and vengeance through their infamous parable. After Lot fled with his wife and daughters as he had been told to do by the angels of deliverance, God annihilated the sinners and wiped their town off the map. However, an interesting study I've read recently suggested that the people of Lot had deserved punishment first and foremost because they never believed in God, and second, because many of them were bandits and rapists. In other words, homosexuality may have not been the sin, or at least not the only sin for which they were destroyed.

I was a little boy when I first heard the word *homosexual*. My parents were commenting on a scene from a film we were watching on television. Two men walked hand in hand to their bedroom, they closed the door behind them, and my father said, "Homosexuals!" I was confused. What did that word mean? In our Arabic culture, men hold each other's hands when they walk; they kiss on the cheek when they meet, and they sometimes hug too. I had seen my father do that with his friends often, so I couldn't understand what was wrong with the scene on television. Why had it embarrassed my folks and made them use that disturbingly long English word?

Growing up and going into high school, our favorite subject of mockery was homosexuality. Like all teenagers, we laughed our heads off at the gestures and slips of tongue that had "gay" connotations. Little did I know then that my closest friend Hassan actually *was* gay.

I first met Hassan at our elementary school. He was my age, only few months younger. He was everybody's favorite and a joy to be around with his endless good humor and cheerful attitude. While the boys made paper pistols and pretended to be gangsters, chasing one another in our school playground, Hassan loved to play double dutch with the girls and could easily beat out the competition. In arts-and-crafts classes, he was exceptionally skillful in sewing, and we once turned an empty bottle of shampoo to a beautifully dressed model. Years later, he became a distinguished pastry chef.

In our high school for boys, things were quite different for Hassan. He had no one to play double dutch with, and the bullying shortly began. He was still affable to many and probably the funniest student in class even though he was becoming more and more flamboyant. Sometimes he didn't mind jokes alluding to his feminine mannerisms. He contributed and even laughed at them. At other times, however, they hurt him so badly that he burst into tears.

After graduating from university and after several arranged engagements that ended in failure, Hassan felt that life in Iraq was suffocating him. His family kept pushing him to get married. His last engagement had only lasted a few months. He told his fiancée, "I'm sorry, but I'm not a real man." Within a few days' time, the news had spread like bushfire and everyone in the city knew about Hassan's *not being a real man.* A couple of months later, Hassan was on his way to Europe with a Schengen visa in his passport. He sneaked into the U.K. and never went back to Iraq.

A few years ago, after a long separation, I met Hassan again in Amman. Grey-haired and wearing thick glasses, he no longer resembled the lively child he once was. He had undergone heart surgery in London. His mother was still nagging him about marriage, and he had seriously considered it because he could no longer stand loneliness. Many girls would not mind marrying gay men these days if it would give them a chance to live in Europe or the States. At that unplanned reunion in Jordan, Hassan and I had a long heart-to-heart talk in which he came out to me. It was my first time discussing homosexuality with a close friend, but it wouldn't be the last.

Scene Three

In an email from my good friend Roula in Paris: *I watched a film that's made my life split in two.* It had been ages since we had last met in Baghdad, but we had kept in touch via email and would occasionally recommend books, films, and music to each other. Roula—half Iraqi, half French—is one of the few people whose art choices I trusted implicitly. *My life is now divided into pre-*A Single Man, *and post-*A Single Man, Roula wrote, and pasted a link to the film's soundtrack by Abel Korzeniowski, whose name I'd never heard before. I started listening to the music on YouTube; the violin laments of "And Just Like That," the first piece I listened to, blew me away. I knew I had to watch the film.

I read a couple of comments online: people said they cried their eyes out during and after the film, and they all agreed that the music was most captivating. The story, based on a novel by Christopher Isherwood, takes place in California during the Cuban Missile Crisis in the sixties. I took a couple of minutes to look at the film's poster outside the cinema. I had never liked Colin Firth, to be honest, and Julianne Moore was not a favorite of mine either, but I went inside anyway.

As the lights dimmed, I stretched my legs and prepared myself for a heart-rending romance between Firth and Moore. I had not the slightest idea that the film was actually about George Falconer, a gay professor grieving the loss of his partner in a car accident and planning to take his own life over it. I was surprised that Roula had never mentioned anything about the gay aspect of the film, and now that I had found out, I couldn't grasp why it had made such an impact on her.

After the film ended, I walked out of the theater with

its music resonating in my head. I knew it would keep haunting me for days afterwards, and it did. I wrote to Roula to thank her for her recommendation. The film was inspiring on so many levels. Its script, to begin with, was thought-provoking. It stirred philosophical questions of love, life, death, and happiness. Depth has sadly become a rare commodity in today's movies, so it was good to find a deep film with substance as opposed to Hollywood's commercial mass production.

The film, directed by renowned fashion designer Tom Ford, was aesthetically executed to perfection. The picture, even at its gloomiest moments, was brilliant and artistic; Firth's performance and Moore's were both outstanding. I was still curious, though, to find out what it was about that specific film that had made Roula, a divorced mother of two (a boy and a girl) consider it a life-changing experience.

Months later, by pure coincidence, I met Roula and got the chance to ask her while we sipped coffee.

"I sent that email to many of my friends, and I didn't mention the homosexual theme on purpose," she said. "I thought you wouldn't take it seriously had I told you beforehand."

I guess Roula was right. I probably wouldn't have bothered to watch the film if I had known about its theme in advance. I still haven't seen *Brokeback Mountain* despite the several prestigious awards it has won and the very good reviews I have read.

"Okay, I understand, but why did it mean that much to

you in the first place?" I couldn't hold back my curiosity any longer.

"Because it touched me profoundly. I've never experienced that type of feelings with a man. I felt jealous of the professor's intense love for his partner. It made me realize how much I've missed out on in my life."

That was a strong statement! Not many Arabs dare to voice their emotional hunger in a culture that molds us to suppress our feelings. I respected Roula's integrity.

I then told her about my own book and my encounter with Rami. I also told her about Hassan and his long struggle with his family. She listened carefully, and then she hit me with yet another unexpected confession: "You know, my little child's school was throwing a masquerade party a few months ago. I asked him what he wanted to dress like, and it really shocked me when he said he wanted to be a princess! It actually took a lot of persuasion to make him change his mind and settle for a prince costume instead." Roula blushed and smiled.

"But what would you do if he came to you one day and said that he was in love with another boy? How would you handle that?" It took some courage for me to pose Rami's hypothetical question to Roula. I probably wouldn't have taken the risk had I not noticed how much she had changed.

I remembered how timid and reserved she had been in Baghdad. It really impressed me how freely she was articulating her feelings now. I knew she had undergone a bitter divorce and was struggling to survive and start a decent new life as a single mother of two children in Paris. Roula was still a practicing Muslim, too. She prayed, fasted, and made sure to avoid alcohol and pork whenever she went out with her friends in the City of Light. After an hour-long conversation at the coffee shop, it was obvious to me that she had developed a different approach to life. She seemed more at ease now and in a way, liberated.

Roula took a deep breath before answering my question (or, to be more precise, my modified version of Rami's): "Well, it's quite hard to explain, but when you love somebody so much, you tend to accept them the way they are." It occurred to me that she might have given thought to the possibility before, and I didn't know what to say. Those words came straight from the heart of a devoted mother. I could not but respect their majesty.

Scene Four

Just before the plane landed at Atatürk International Airport in Istanbul, and while I was browsing through a Turkish newspaper, I saw a photo that really struck me: a nightclub's advertisement had a large picture of a young man in a two-piece belly-dance costume. I couldn't understand a word—it was all in Turkish—but the picture seemed weird to me. In the Arab world, men don't belly dance. Only female dancers would wear such colorful costumes.

The next morning, I started looking for a small studio in the old city. I knocked on the door and an old lady wearing *hijab* opened. I told her I was interested in renting her property. She said, "It's a nice place, you will love it. We have a homosexual prostitute living next door, though. But don't worry, he's friendly and harmless."

Of course, I was well aware that Turkey was different from its Islamic surrounds. I just didn't expect it to be *that* different! I saw many Turks in the streets of Istanbul in traditional Islamic clothing, working and living side by side with other Turks who were decked out in the latest European fashions. I saw Muslim girls in extremely tiny skirts and low-cut tops wearing small Islamic pendants around their necks while drinking in bars and enjoying casual relationships. A young man in a short girly dress passed me by. He had long blond hair and makeup on his face. Another cultural shock.

If anything, that trip in 1995 introduced me to a politically secular country with a majority Muslim population that seemed to tolerate and even accept open homosexuality. At first, I thought it was an exception to the rule, but after reading several history books, I realized Turkey might not be the only example of its kind. I found stories about several Muslim rulers and poets who had openly proclaimed their sexuality, and I was flabbergasted when I read some of the erotic poems they had written for their male lovers and slaves only a few centuries after the Prophet's death!

Scene Five

In order to give a balanced account of Muslim homosexuals, I thought I should talk about intimate relations between Muslim women too, but it was hard to find access to information given the high walls of secrecy surrounding the topic. Muslim women don't usually open up about these things, especially not with a male stranger.

My first knowledge of romance and sex between women came not very long after I'd found out about male homosexuality. I was listening to our beloved nanny one day while she gossiped with my mother about some ladies said to have had liaisons with other women. The two of them, my mother and nanny, laughed at those stories, but I didn't. I didn't get the joke.

I knew those ladies very well. They visited us in our house, and even as a child, I'd always admired their refined demeanor and the great respect everyone had paid them. They were distinguished socialites, married or widowed with sons and grandsons. They prayed, fasted, fed the poor and needy, and if I remember well, they all had gone to Mecca at least once. However, people were circulating rumors about the women-only Turkish baths one of those ladies had taken to hosting in her own house, where guests were welcome to stay overnight and be treated to lavish buffet dinners and breakfasts. Now except for the overnight stay, which was not so familiar to me, I couldn't see what was wrong with having guests in the house. I mean, women-only events have always been popular in our society. My mother had frequently invited her female friends to brunch, lunch, or dinner in our house. I remember she worked hard to impress her guests with new table decorations and food selections. However, it wasn't until years later that I learned not all the ladies' events were as innocent as my mother's.

I'd also known a few tomboys. They dressed like men, cut their hair short, and would not hesitate to beat the hell out of anyone who dared to taunt them. Most of those girls never got married, but not marrying can't really be a proof of homosexuality. Actually, it's really hard to say who is gay and who is not in an Arab-Muslim environment where men and women hang out, travel, and dine with friends of the same gender all the time. It's the social norm in this part of the world.

Still wanting to know more, I decided to go online to talk with Arab lesbians in chat rooms. The thing is, when you talk with someone online, you can't really be sure of his or her true identity, so you might end up talking to a bearded hunk that, for some reason, finds pleasure in pretending to be a young lesbian girl. I couldn't find anyone there who was willing to go through the topic seriously. All they were interested in was to have webcam sex. After a few attempts, I dumped the whole idea. Lesbian chat rooms were definitely not the right place to find the information I sought. I managed to find a few blogs by Arab lesbian girls, but they too used pseudonyms, which raised serious concerns about the credibility of their stories. Unless by some chance I get to meet a lesbian girl who agrees to speak freely about it someday, the world of Arab lesbians will remain a mystery to me.

Scene Six

If I were asked to name the chief benefit of the war on Iraq in 2003, I would probably say it was allowing the Iraqis to communicate freely with the rest of the world, although I'm not sure if it was really worth the mighty cost. But since the price had been paid already, I decided to make the most of it. For over two years after the war, I dedicated much of my time to surfing the web. I had a thirst for knowledge and information. I needed to meet people of different cultures, religions, and views of life. I wanted to experience political debates without fear, something I'd never tried before.

During Saddam's rule, all Internet cafés were put under strict surveillance and most political sites were blocked. After the war, everything changed. Despite the mass destruction of power stations throughout the country and the absence of electricity, millions of households began to obtain satellite receivers, cell phones, and other electronic gadgets. Both importers and retailers made record profits from the boom of modern technology in newly liberated Iraq.

I didn't have Internet access at home in the beginning, so I used to go to the net café near my house. Each time I tried to search something on Google, just as I typed the letter G into the browsing bar, a long list of gay sites would unfold on the screen. This happened every time, and it meant only one thing: there were neighbors sitting in my seat, watching and enjoying the material those sites provided. That incident made me realize for the first time that we had several homosexuals in our neighborhood. I have to say, it was a quite an unexpected finding.

Scene Seven

Our online correspondence lasted a long time before my Egyptian friend Ahmed, a brilliant student of literature and one of the politest men I have ever known, decided to share his biggest secret with me. During our virtual acquaintance, I had noticed that he got defensive each time we discussed religion. He didn't mind political arguments and had impressively liberal views there. But when it came to discussing the fundamentals of religion, or even their controversial interpretations, he tensed up and refused to listen. I had a feeling he was trying to prove something to himself. I had no idea what it was, though.

Ahmed sounded really distressed one day: "I despise myself. I wish to die." He needed to open up to a friend who would not misjudge him, or even better, would not judge him at all. Also, the two of us being online friends may have made talking much easier for him. "My agony makes me cry bitter tears every night," he elaborated. "I'm sexually different. I lust for men." I was speechless. For someone as conventionally religious as himself, having to live with homosexuality must have been excruciating.

"I was bullied when I was a child. It was an older boy in school. I remember I didn't run away when he started hitting me. I was bleeding, but I neither shouted nor cried. I didn't even try to defend myself. Even at that young age, I had great faith in God. I was talking to God, and I told Him, *I know you are watching over me. I know you will come to my rescue. Please don't leave me alone here!*" I read Ahmed's lines on the screen with tearful eyes and felt goose bumps rising on my arms. I've never met anyone who trusted in God like that child from the poor village on the bank of the river Nile did. He stood trance-like, his body battered and bruised while his soul was communing with God.

Ahmed was convinced that the bullying he'd suffered

when he was a child had resulted in his becoming a homosexual. It may or may not have been the reason. Although there are several theories, the real cause of homosexuality has not been conclusively determined yet. Whether it's determined by genetics or prenatal hormones or environmental factors, or maybe multiple factors, no one really knows.

Among several interesting explanations I have found is one suggesting that homosexuality is a by-product of strict religiousness in communities that worship a male god. Christianity, for instance, has been celebrating an idealistic image of women based on virginity and motherhood alone, nothing carnal whatsoever. Christian cathedrals and churches are packed with icons and statues of naked Jesus nailed to the cross, and Christian children grow up praying to a male figure. They are taught to beg for his love, which they do wholeheartedly, and as a result, many of them end up desiring men.

This analysis falls short of answering questions like why homosexuals exist in non-Christian and polytheistic countries too, and why all Christian men aren't homosexuals, having been exposed to the same stimulus during childhood. Also, what about Christian lesbians? What could have shaped their sexual orientation?

Scene Eight

In video footage that leaked from the archives of the General Security Directorate in Baghdad after the war, I saw a trembling young man accused of homosexuality being thrown off a multi-storey building. Of course, the possibility remains that the executed man in the film was not even gay. He could have been a political opponent whom the authorities then had decided to condemn, along with his family, to eternal ignominy. But either way, homosexual or not, no one deserves to die in that horrible way. Punishments against homosexuals vary from one Muslim country to another. While there is no penalty for homosexual acts in Turkish law, they may be punished by imprisonment in Egypt and flogging in Malaysia. And in countries like Saudi Arabia and Iran, homosexuals, especially those caught doing sodomy, can be sentenced to death.

Following in the steps of European countries like Holland and Belgium, several American states have recognized same-sex marriage and allowed adoption by same-sex couples. The Presbyterian Church now allows openly gay men and women to be ordained as clergy, and they have recently been permitted to serve in the armed forces too, but that doesn't mean all Americans back gay rights. I once had an interesting chat with an American friend about the subject. Brad said that people should be free to pursue their sexual desires as long as they didn't offend other people, but the thing with homosexuals in the United States was that they didn't stop there.

"After every recognition they receive, they immediately start campaigning for more and more rights!" Brad went on. "They will not rest until they've brought about the complete abolition of the Christian culture of this country." Well, I don't know about American homosexuals, but I do know that's not the case with the Muslim homosexuals, or at least not the few I've met so far.

It's highly unlikely that Muslim lawmakers will bring in pro-gay legislation similar to what is available in the West in the near future. Actually, if there will be any legal changes, they'd further harden the already existing punishments. But severe punishments may be nothing compared to the nonstop self-inflicted torment most Muslim gays endure. Rami, Ahmed, and Hassan all hate themselves. They beat themselves up all the time over the way they feel, but that's not all. They spend their lives pretending to be people they are not. Deep inside, they know they are lying, and it consumes much of their energy. Even when they have sex or mentally indulge in their fantasies, Muslim gays are constantly inhabited by feelings of guilt and shame. Many of those men and women are cultivated and talented, but rarely can they reach their full potential because as human beings, they are never in their entirety. They are only fractions of their true selves, and that in itself is a psychological torture, probably more agonizing than any physical punishment.

Scene Nine

"I know you are different," I told Hassan. We hadn't talked about his sexual orientation before. Of course I had heard people gossip about it after he'd broken up with his first fiancée, but he never admitted it to me. It didn't really matter. Hassan will always be my good childhood friend. I didn't see why his sexual orientation should in any way disturb our long-standing friendship. I wanted him to know that, and he appreciated it. Hassan has such a good heart; he's always been kind to everyone, and he trusts people infinitely. Even when some of his friends turned on him and stabbed him in the back, he didn't hurt them back. He loved to look after old people and play with children, and he would never hesitate to nurse a sick friend. It's really hard to think that God will ignore all the goodness in Hassan's soul and burn him in hell just for being who he is.

CHAPTER 6

The Patriarch's Conversion

WHEN THE NIGHT FELL ON HIM, HE SAW A
STAR. HE SAID: THIS IS MY LORD. BUT AS IT
SET, HE SAID: I LOVE NOT THINGS THAT SET.
AND WHEN HE SAW THE MOON RISING, HE
SAID: THIS IS MY LORD. BUT AS IT SET, HE SAID:
UNLESS MY LORD GUIDES ME, I SHALL BE ONE
OF THE ASTRAY. AND THEN WHEN HE SAW
THE SUN RISING, HE SAID: THIS IS MY LORD,
THIS IS GREATER. BUT AS IT SET, HE SAID: O
MY PEOPLE, I DISAVOW YOUR INFIDELITY. I
HAVE TURNED STRAIGHT TO HIM, HE WHO
CREATED THE HEAVENS AND THE EARTH, AND
I SHALL NEVER BE OF THE PAGANS AGAIN.

(6.76,77,78,79)

In Arabic, we rarely say someone has converted to Islam. I don't know if this is a coincidence or one of those instances in language where terms tend to reflect people's collective subconscious. Even the Christians in the Arab world don't say that because the only connotation *conversion* conveys is dishonorable and cowardly. Most people would say they've embraced Islam or have become Muslims.

I chose the above verses because they depict the

moments of conversion in the life of a young man who'd later become the founding patriarch of all the monotheistic faiths we know today.

Scene One

Uncle Saad's life was turned upside down after he was diagnosed with cancer. My father's dear friend was clearly distressed when I last saw him. As if he'd become a totally different person, the once-eloquent speaker sat quiet in his living room, barely uttering a word. I tried to distract him from his sorrow by asking him about his latest readings. He'd always been fond of history books, and he used to give me excellent reviews of them. He read them in Arabic, English, and French.

"I only read the Holy Koran now. I stopped reading other books." His voice came out weak. Not knowing what to say, I tried to put a smile on my face.

All Uncle Saad's life, he had been a secular man. He had travelled the world and had lots of friends everywhere. His wife Leila was a socialite too. She drove her own car, drank, and smoked openly, but that wasn't uncommon among women in her social circle.

"Since his sickness, he's become obsessed with religion. He says it comforts him," Leila confided to me when her husband left the room to take some pills.

I stayed there for a short time and then left to catch up with other friends. On my way back home, I had many thoughts nagging me. After long decades of being an unobservant Muslim, this man's life had changed drastically, and religion was now his only solace. Would it have been possible for this conversion to take place had some fanatic executed him years ago while he wasn't this devout? I couldn't help but wonder.

Scene Two

"Bloody communist!" I was too young to know what that word meant, but like all children I was able to recognize curses from the way they sounded rather than their actual meanings. My parents were talking about a man my father knew then. He must have done or said something that made them upset and qualified him for the *bloody* title. Several years later, I realized the cursed man was not the only communist my parents had known. There actually had been others, both males and females.

Before and during the mid-twentieth century, many Arab intellectuals fell under the spell of the rising communist movement and its idealistic slogans and promises of justice, equality, and fair distribution of wealth. Most of those enthusiastic men and women bore Islamic names and descended from devout families, but that didn't stop them from embracing the new atheist doctrine that conflicted sharply with the religious and cultural legacy of their ancestors. Supported by the Soviet Union, they established local communist parties throughout the Arab world, staged coups d'état here and there, and eventually managed to have a considerable amount of political clout in several countries, including Iraq.

On the other hand, the majority of people remained rooted in their Islamic heritage and refused to compromise their faith at any cost. It soon became obvious to everyone that religion was the main obstacle against the spread of communism, a fact that was cunningly exploited by communism's capitalist adversaries to hinder its growth in this critical part of the world.

Although my parents, not religious then, were among the many Iraqis who instinctively rejected communism, they did have a few friends with leftist inclinations. After the fall of the Berlin Wall in 1989 and the dramatic collapse of the Soviet Union, everything changed in the blink of an eye. The old comrades fell into depression. They saw their big dreams crushed; they felt useless and redundant. Some chose to seclude themselves from the world, spending the rest of their lives recollecting memories of a passionate past, while others decided to turn their backs on it all. They discarded their old books and sought repentance from God for their atheist years. They prayed day and night and hardly put the Koran down. I was there, witnessing their transformation. This experience was quite enlightening because it made me realize the changeable nature of life and people at a reasonably early age.

Scene Three

In the Koran, God threatens to punish apostates by burning them in eternal hell in the afterlife. If everything in the afterlife is God's business and His alone, what about this earthly life? How are Muslims supposed to handle cases of apostasy in this current time? I'm afraid there is a lot of confusion in this area as well. While some verses clearly state that there should be no compulsion in religion, other verses prescribe—or seem to prescribe—the killing of apostates. And while I've read that the Prophet tolerated several cases of conversion during his life, I've also found some sayings that condemn conversion. In any case, apostasy today is illegal and punishable by death in many Islamic countries. But things don't get that far, usually.

Hardly anyone—or at least no one that I'm aware of—has declared apostasy in court and accepted legal responsibility for it. There is absolutely no advantage in doing so. Not even fervent Arab communists did that. Their personal documents still said they were Muslims even when they weren't. Most converts would keep their beliefs to themselves and their trusted circle of friends instead of taking the matter to an official and unnecessarily life-threatening level.

I find the very premise of punishing people for transforming their faith contradictory to both common sense and the teachings of Islam. First and foremost, there is no use in forcing religion on people because unless it comes through true conviction, religion is a mere mask. And God is definitely not concerned about masks. Second, God could have saved us the trouble of searching for the truth had He wanted us to have it the easy way, but He didn't. Instead, He made it a lifetime quest that involves a lot of thinking and contemplation. Thinking is the only mechanism for humans to make choices in life, including our choices to adopt a new faith or return to an original one. Both are changes, and I believe every change is a conversion.

Also, in the Koran, God repeatedly urges believers to ponder over themselves and the world around them. I actually do that all the time, and my pondering has led me to the conclusion that it's impossible for human beings to stand still in an ever-changing universe. Seasons change, birds migrate, the moon eclipses, and earthquakes and hurricanes strike. Humans love and hate; we sin, repent, and sin again. Conversion manifests itself inside and around each one of us in an endless variety.

Scene Four

There have been times of conversion in my life. When I was young and confused, I couldn't see the point of having to live my whole life as a Muslim just because I was born into a Muslim family, so I decided to rebel. No one knew about my conversions, not even my friends or family. Looking back, I'm not sure if they were actual conversions or just periods of uncertainty. I had so many doubts in my head. I tried to find answers in the Koran but could not get much. I sought help from God, but He seemed remote, uninterested. I felt so abandoned that I once opened the window and shouted to the sky, "You are unfair!"

Oddly enough, those short bursts of agnosticism were followed by periods of deep religiosity. When I read the Koran, every line there seemed to be talking to me. I felt God was so close that I could hear His voice and touch His hand. I thought I had finally found what I was looking for. But doubts would rise again, and I kept swinging between skepticism and faith for quite a long time. Even at my age now, I still harbor qualms about God and religion from time to time, but I don't think this is a bad thing. These unvoiced phases of war and peace are essential for our spiritual growth, regardless of which creed we may choose to adopt.

If pressed to give a definition of wisdom, mine would entail taking time off to look at life outside the narrow circle of mainstream norms and traditions, to try to figure out where it's leading me, why, and whether I really want to go there.

While some people choose to sail away to explore new horizons, others choose to go back to their old herds. It would be a conscious return, though, a free choice based on personal conviction, but better than blindly following in the footsteps of others. All through the history of mankind, trial and error have resulted in some of the most brilliant inventions. And thousands of years ago in southern Iraq, it was trial and error that led a young and confused Abraham to the knowledge of the One God, which would eventually change the perception of deity for billions of humans once and for all.

CHAPTER 7

Golden Domes, Secret Prisons, and Sticky Sweets

AND AL MASAJID (THE MOSQUES) ARE GOD'S,
SO CALL UPON NONE OTHER THAN HIM.
(72.18)

Masjid, the Arabic word for *mosque*, is derived from the verb *sajada* (to prostrate). It refers to the temple where Islamic group prayers are carried out five times a day in addition to other seasonal prayers conducted during the nights of Ramadan and shortly after sunrise on the two Islamic holidays. These short prayers are performed without bowing, kneeling, or prostration during funerals (funeral prayer is another type of prayer sometimes performed in the mosque).

I just thought a brief etymological introduction would be necessary before approaching the first scene. A pinch of conspiracy theory to start with!

Scene One

It had been quite a while since I last heard from Firas. We first met during our eighteen-month compulsory military service. We spent most of that time together, but when it was over, we went our separate ways and never had the chance to meet again. I heard he had gotten married, had two sons, and then left Iraq amongst thousands of young engineers, who—under compelling circumstances during the nineties—had packed up and fled the country. Luckily enough, Firas managed to find a decent job in Saudi Arabia with the help of some family acquaintances. Our mutual friends told me that he'd become religious: "He grew a long beard and made his wife cover. They both went on pilgrimage to Mecca."

I wasn't surprised to hear that, honestly. First, Mecca is only an hour's drive from Jeddah, where Firas was working and living with his family. And second, it's only natural for an observant Muslim to fulfill the fifth pillar of faith, pilgrimage. Actually, Firas wasn't the first person I knew who had become pious. Several other friends have turned to religion, and I've taught myself to respect people's personal choices as long as they don't violate mine. Firas's religiosity was by no means a threat to my liberalism, so I didn't see why I should mind it, or even care.

Very Important, read the subject line of an email I received from Firas one day. I thought it could be virus-infected or a spam, but the subject had a tempting completion: *Every Muslim must read this!* I decided to take the risk, and much to my surprise, the letter started with what looked like a riddle: *Do you know where the English word* mosque *comes from?*

I immediately recalled my old search for the word's roots in my school library. We didn't have the Internet then, so books were our only means to access information. All the books I had read there confirmed my initial conjecture about the obvious phonetic resemblance between *masjid* and *mosque* especially in their first syllables. According to these sources, the Iberian Peninsula was the first soil the Muslim armies had trodden upon in their European conquest in the early eighth century, and *mosque* had been modified from the Spanish name given to Muslim temples: *mezquitas*. The email I received from Firas didn't deny the Spanish origin of the word, yet it had a totally different story to convey:

> I was flipping through an interesting book which pointed out that the English word *mosque* was derived from the Spanish *mosquito* during the reign of King Ferdinand II who'd spoken to his soldiers upon one of their crusades saying, 'I will go and swat the Muslims like mosquitoes.' The narrative made my blood boil as I'm sure it will make yours too, my dear fellow Muslims. This story I'm telling you here, my brothers and sisters in God, is only a reminder of the hatred towards all Muslims that fills the hearts of those infidels. The Ummah should not be deceived by their lies of tolerance and respect for Islam for the seeds of jealousy and malice against our religion had long been sown in their hearts. Therefore, we all should immediately refrain from using that humiliating word and replace it with our beautiful Arabic word *masjid*. I urge you hereby to forward this email to all your contacts to help us removing that ugly stigma.

The letter ended with a verse (I don't remember which one it was) from the Koran about the ill intentions of the nonbelievers.

My Google search only took a few seconds to get heaps of results. I read the first few carefully, and they all supported my previous conclusion. I also found several results confirming that *mosque* was already in use long before King Ferdinand II was even born.

Firas's forwarded letter was the first in a series of similar *high alert* emails that began pouring into my inbox from my newly devout friends. After reading a few, it became easy for me to predict the structure and content of each message just by reading its title. They all claimed to have found a new conspiracy against Islam and the Muslims. Their numbers increased so much that I had no other choice but to send them straight to my junk folder. I still feel a twinge of guilt about it.

Scene Two

Just when I thought I'd lost them forever, memories of my first time in a mosque came back to me as intermittent flashes loaded with colors, scents, voices, and flavors, taking me back to my childhood and making me relive my enthusiasm for that trip all over again. My parents had all of a sudden decided to take us to visit the Shia shrines south of Baghdad. Our outing felt like a picnic rather than a pilgrimage. At that time—I keep saying this—most people had a lenient and flexible sense of religion. They didn't take it as seriously as they do nowadays. So yes, we were going on a picnic.

My memories of the trip smell of burning incense. It was impossible for anyone in the shrine, let alone a little child, to ignore such an intriguing scent. From the main gate to the marble courtyard and the prayer hall, the air was rich with a smoky wood fragrance. It must have been springtime: the air felt warm, not hot, and the sun shone brightly. Like a sea of shimmering diamonds, the broken-mirror mosaic on the walls reflected the sunlight coming through the dome, illuminating the place. The sight of it filled me with a strange sense of awe and wonder. My memories also bear the sound of humming and whispers, for no one was allowed to raise their voice in the shrine. Only the call to noon prayer was permitted to interrupt the quiet of the place. I remember the call was loud, so loud that it startled me.

My memories also taste of hard toffee. Just before we left the city, my parents took us to the local market and bought us some traditional candies, *sahoon*. They had the tantalizing color of milk chocolate, and I was so hungry that I put all the pieces in my mouth. Unlike milk chocolate, *sahoon* was surprisingly hard. I felt like I was chewing broken glass. I was too embarrassed to spit out the pieces, so I let them melt and ooze their rich sweetness. Suddenly I couldn't chew anymore. The candy had glued my mouth shut! I had to wait a good while until it dissolved, releasing my stuck jaws. It was a terrible feeling, and I never ate *sahoon* again after that.

Ironically, though I can't find anything about praying in

my memories. I was only a little boy, and I didn't even know *how* to pray. But I remember well that my father, who is keen on not missing a single prayer now, never really cared to pray then. He stayed outside, smoking in the courtyard. Actually, I'm pretty sure no one in my family prayed at the shrine that day. We spent most of the time hanging around the old market.

Scene Three

My second time in a mosque was quite different. As I said earlier, I was taught to pray in elementary school but my home prayers had become a regular chore by then. I prayed so fast that I couldn't have paid much attention to the verses I was reciting. There was always something interesting on television I didn't want to miss. My friend and I felt that we had outgrown praying at home, so it was about time that we tried our first group prayer at a renowned Sunni shrine not very far from our houses. I had no concern whatsoever for denominational differences. I didn't even know they existed.

As the imam finished reciting the first chapter (*Surat Al-Fatiha*, or The Opening) of the Koran—a supplication for guidance and salvation, we all answered in one voice: *Amen*. A sudden shudder of cold passed over me. The sound resonated beautifully throughout the hall. I wanted my prayer to last forever. I had never expected my first group prayer to feel so good. Engulfed by tranquility, I hardly paid attention to details because my excursion felt like a pilgrimage this time. I did notice though that the architecture of the Sunni shrine was almost identical to that of the

Shia shrine I'd visited with my family when I was a little child. The dome, the minarets, mirrored walls, crystal chandeliers, Persian rugs, all the silver and gold ornaments, and even the smell of incense and the loud call to prayer with its grieving tone (to which I'd grown accustomed) had all become familiar to me.

Sadly, my spiritual exhilaration wasn't meant to last long. My friend and I decided to go for a short walk after prayer. It was summertime and the air was exceptionally cool that night. Right next to us was a beautiful park overlooking the river Tigris—which, I have to admit, did seem strangely quiet and desolate, but we didn't care. No sooner had we walked inside than we saw dark shadows surrounding us from every direction.

"Freeze!" one of the shadows shouted as he shone a blinding light in our panicked eyes. We heard the rattle of machine guns being pointed at us. "Who are you and what are you doing here?"

Taken aback, I gasped, "We're just walking around. Is there something wrong?"

He ignored my naïve question and demanded to see our identification. Thank God we had our school cards with us. Our hands trembled as we handed them to him.

"They're students," he told someone on the radio. The other man's voice was barely discernible, or maybe I was too confused to decipher what he'd been saying. After a while, they realized how foolish and innocent we were, ordering us to leave and never come back to the park again. We walked as fast as we could while their lights were still spotted on our backs. We couldn't believe they had finally let us go. Although our ordeal only lasted thirty minutes, it seemed like an eternity. Still shaking, we took a taxi back home, kept silent all the way, and never dared to utter a single word about it, not even to our parents. In fact, this may be my first time telling the story to anyone.

I recalled those terrifying moments again when I read in the newspaper that American soldiers had heard cries and moans coming from cellars full of prisoners underneath that park in 2003. They also claimed to have found ghastly torture chambers with horrifying killing machines, including a huge shredder into which political dissidents had been regularly fed. It chewed up their bodies and ejected their minced remains into the Tigris. I don't know for certain about that machine, and despite doubts later surfacing in the media about whether it had really existed, I wouldn't be surprised if it did. I'm pretty sure something creepy had been going on when we walked into the park. Just thinking about how close I had come to that prison and that I had actually trodden on its terrain gives me a chill.

The memory of my second time in a mosque will always hold an ambiance of fear. Instead of thanking God for saving my life and my friend's, I felt betrayed and let down. When I went to bed that night, my earlier mosque-prayer bliss had faded almost to nothing. I remember asking God, *Why did you let that happen just when I thought you were listening to me and would guide and protect me?* Frustration took over and stopped me from praying at the mosque again for many months.

Scene Four

When I was in Baghdad, one of my favorite day excursions was exploring the serpentine alleys of the old city. Each time I went there, the air was filled with music played by architecture. Traditional houses with their brick walls, enclosed balconies, and colorful latticed windows conducted a symphony of light and shade that was as vivid and compelling as Beethoven's music, or Bach's. Just writing about that sensation now makes me yearn to live it again.

Almost one year after I left Iraq, I received an email from a friend working in Abu Dhabi. It had a slideshow of the Grand Sheikh Zayed Mosque. I was curious to peek at the half-billion-dollar monument named after the late Sheikh Zayed Al Nahyan, the founder of the United Arab Emirates, who in 2004 was buried in the courtyard of the new mosque while it was still under construction. The mosque had been making the news with several of its record-breaking features, among which was the world's largest chandelier—made of copper and plated in twenty-four-carat gold, imported from Germany and decorated with thousands of Swarovski crystals. It also had the world's largest Persian carpet, exclusively woven by Iran Carpet Company. Over a thousand highly skilled Iranian weavers at a workshop in Khorasan made the almost-six-thousand-square-meter green rug. And last but not least, the mosque's main dome was believed to be the largest of its kind worldwide.

As I looked at the images on my monitor, I thought, *That's theme-park architecture!* The interior design would not have looked out of place in the Arabian Pavilion at

Disney's Millennium Village in Orlando, Florida, or even in the lobby of an *Arabian-Nights*-themed hotel in Las Vegas. But a mosque? It was impossible to keep the crouching critic in me on a tight leash any longer.

According to its website, the Sheikh Zayed Mosque is able to accommodate more than forty thousand worshippers. I must say it's a bit ironic that in a small country like the UAE with a population of less than five million—almost eighty percent of whom are foreign residents—stands one of the largest mosques in the world. It competes with the Badshahi Mosque in Lahore and the Jama Masjid in Old Delhi, despite the fact that Pakistan and India have an estimated Muslim population of more than three hundred and forty million—that is, almost twenty percent of the world's total Muslim populace.

But size is definitely not the project's only prodigality. The mosque has a huge artificial lake; four massive minarets on its four corners; and over a thousand marble columns, approximately a hundred of which stand in the main prayer hall decorated with semi-precious stones, mother of pearl, and twenty-four-carat gold. Dozens of white marble domes roof the structure, and thousands of meters of colored floral marble patterns pave its floors.

I haven't visited the Grand Sheikh Zayed Mosque in Abu Dhabi yet. It would be interesting to experience the monument's opulent atmosphere firsthand one day. But looking at its pictures online reveals a screaming lack of unity, probably due to the fact that there was no chief designer of the project. *Sheikh Zayed Grand Mosque seeks to achieve positive interaction with other cultures*, says its website. Unfortunately, the final product of such interaction came out as an odd mélange of conflicting styles and patterns: Arabic calligraphy, European Renaissance, and Art Deco ornaments, in addition to evident Mogul influences—mainly on the exteriors—and a pinch of Andalusian and Ottoman arts. As I browsed through more images, I had this strange feeling that I was listening to a huge orchestra with all instruments being played all at the same time. Moreover, I'm not sure if the main prayer hall is even functional... unless worshippers inside the mosque close their eyes. Otherwise, they will undoubtedly have a hard time focusing on prayer with all the visual distraction surrounding them.

The Hassan II Mosque in Casablanca is another dazzling Islamic monument I have scrutinized online. It was built on a promontory that looks out to the Atlantic Ocean. The mosque's spectacular maritime view is unique, likewise its glass flooring, which enables people inside to bow and kneel directly over the water. The Moroccan landmark named after the late King Hassan II is able to host over a hundred thousand worshippers and has the world's tallest minaret at a height of more than two hundred meters, but this is apt to change sometime soon. The competition has become extremely fierce with a new North African contender entering the chart.

Algeria—Morocco's regional and traditional rival, still recovering from long years of civil conflict—is constructing the Algiers Mosque, which will be inaugurated as the third-largest mosque in the world, after the mosques of Mecca and

Medina in Saudi Arabia. The religious complex is a multi-
billion-dollar project featuring a wide variety of facilities.
Its two-hundred-and-seventy-meter-high minaret tower
will be the tallest and largest in the world, outshining that
of King Hassan's mosque in Morocco.

The budget-draining war of the minarets has raged
on, irrespective of the high percentage of people living in
poverty. In Iraq, for instance, a mosque extravaganza took
place while child mortality rates were rising due to malnutrition and disease. Until just a few months before the war
in 2003, construction was underway on gigantic mosques
in Baghdad and other Iraqi cities. The biggest of these was
the Grand Saddam Mosque: had it been completed, it was
expected to surpass both the Holy Mosque in Mecca and
the Prophet's Mosque in Medina in size.

I often wonder if Allah really wants this. Gold, silver,
crystal, marble, silk, high minarets, and huge domes: do
we need all of that to talk to God? Wouldn't He listen to
us if we prayed at home or in the silence of the wilderness? Hadn't He sent Gabriel the Archangel to speak to
Mohammed when he was meditating in the dark and desolate cave of Hira? Oddly enough, I would get the answer to
my questions in a small prayer room in Abu Dhabi, the very
city that prides itself for hosting the most opulent mosque
in the world.

Scene Five

While touring Thailand in 1990, I grabbed the opportunity to visit Bangkok's Wat Pho, the Temple of the

Reclining Buddha, where an enormous statue of Buddha passing into nirvana was erected in the early nineteenth century. I still remember the feeling I had as I walked around the gold-plated monument with nacre inlay on the eyes and the soles of the feet. *I'm actually circling an idol!* I couldn't help thinking. The statue, forty-six meters long and fifteen meters high, reminded me of the idols I'd seen in old Arabic films about the rise of Islam. Though, this time, it was humongous.

I had read a few books about Buddha, or Siddhartha, the young prince who'd turned his back on the material world, leaving behind luxurious palaces to wander in the wilderness and seek enlightenment by way of asceticism and dispossession. This very same person was there in front of me, depicted in standing, sitting, and reclining statues cast in gold and precious emeralds, located at massive temples built to commemorate his transcendental spiritual journey. I found that quite ironic, although I must admit similar thoughts crossed my mind when I saw the Vatican on television. The poignant sculpture of the gaunt and semi-naked Jesus nailed to the cross and wearing a crown of thorns contradicted the sumptuousness of the place and the overly embroidered and colorful vestments of the Pope praying beneath.

The paradox is not limited to Buddhism and Christianity. It manifests itself as well in several colossal mosques. All the books I've read about the life of Mohammed say that he led a life of renunciation. Except for his several marriages, he hardly had any known worldly lusts. He was often seen with

stones tied on his stomach to help him endure his pangs
of hunger (having given food away to the poor). He slept
on the floor, wore the humblest of garments, and despised
riches and abundance despite the fact that he had the
treasury of the state at his disposal. When he died in 632,
Mohammed's possessions were a white mule, a sword, and a
piece of land. All of which were distributed to charity.

The proclivity to lavishness and exhibitionism, however,
started showing up after the Prophet's death, or to be more
precise, after the death of the fourth Caliph in 661. By then,
the Islamic state had become a vast empire with massive
revenues. Huge palaces, mosques, and shrines were built.
The spiritual creed was transformed into a materialistic
civilization, where extravagance became synonymous with
power, and where asceticism and humility would no longer
suffice.

Whether it's a dome, a minaret, or even gilded verses
from the Koran decorating the interior, exterior, or both,
gold—the color, and in many cases the very mineral—
has become a must-have element in almost every existing
mosque. Its ancient, yet not genuine, association with Islam
can be observed through an annual ritual that takes place
during the season of pilgrimage to Mecca. The Ka'ba, the
black stone building towards which all Muslims pray, is
covered each year with a new garment made from tons of
pure white silk, dyed black and woven in a special local
factory. More than two hundred specially trained craftsmen
then embroider the cloth with gold and silver threads

depicting an elegant cornice of verses at an estimated cost of five million American dollars.

During the days of the Prophet, the Ka'ba was covered with plain, modest clothing, neither gilt nor silvered. Its single wooden door was coated with gold and silver in the centuries after the Prophet's death; it is now cast in solid gold. I understand of course that Saudi Arabia is a rich country, and I understand that there are Arab tycoons who don't mind losing five million dollars in one night gambling in Beirut, Las Vegas, or Monte Carlo. But I also know that a hundred dollars can feed an entire family for a whole month in a city like Gaza, where nearly seventy percent of people live below the poverty line, and that as little as one dollar per day can make a big difference in a Muslim family's life in Somalia, Sudan, or any of the several Islamic states on the United Nations' review of the world's least-developed countries.

The First Mosques

In the year 622, the Prophet commanded the construction of the first mosque in Islam at the outskirts of Yethrib. It is said that Mohammed had actually participated in building the Quba Mosque, where he stayed for a few days before moving on to build another mosque in what was yet to be called his city, Medina.

The first two mosques had several features in common: they both had a square space for conducting prayers, keeping in mind that the Muslims were first instructed to pray facing Jerusalem until the Prophet received another revelation to turn towards Mecca almost a year and a half after he had fled to Medina. Surrounded by four adobe walls, each prayer yard was partly thatched with mud-plastered palm fronds. The interwoven roofs rested on palm trunks and used to leak rainwater and mud during the winter. Those mosques were quickly constructed using cheap local materials and building techniques to meet a very basic and timely need. Embellishments and ornaments couldn't have been afforded at the time.

The Medina Mosque became Mohammed's residence and court as well, and would double in size in just a few years. When the Prophet died almost a decade later, his body was buried there to consecrate the place as the second holiest site for all Muslims. The mosque has undergone consecutive renovations and expansions over the ensuing fourteen centuries. It can now accommodate almost a million pilgrims during peak seasons, and it occupies almost the entire area of the original city as it was when Mohammed first set foot there. Sadly though, the feeble walls of the original mosque have long since tumbled down, and there are hardly any remainders left today of its first structure.

Metamorphosis

Minarets and domes have been shaping the skylines of Islamic cities for ages, adding their mystical appeal to the sunrise and sunset panorama. Baghdad alone has hundreds of them, and Cairo has a reputation for being the "city with one thousand minarets." Having said that, it might be surprising to know that it wasn't until seven decades after the construction of the first mosque in Medina that a dome was built atop a mosque, the Dome of the Rock Mosque in Jerusalem. Islam was becoming a regional power, expanding in every direction. Mosques were expected to provide large, protected praying areas for the hundreds and thousands of worshippers attending prayers. Domes seemed like a perfect solution because they could enclose large, column-free spaces underneath them. The Byzantines had already adopted and developed dome structures when Muslim armies conquered the Levant, and it is believed that the Muslim architects of the time emulated them.

There was also a need to make the call to prayer audible to the largest number of people possible. The solution was to build a tower in every mosque for the prayer-caller or *muezzin* to climb and sound the call far and wide. While many historians reckon that Byzantine church towers influenced Islamic minarets, there are strong indications that they in turn influenced several cathedrals built in Europe after the defeat of the Muslim armies in the tenth century. Such interesting architectural exchanges can be detected throughout the territories that experienced Islamic conquest in North Africa and Asia.

I once attempted to climb up a famous minaret in Baghdad. I was writing an assignment on traditional mosques and needed to take some photographs of the minaret's balcony. After climbing a dozen stairs, my enthusiasm started dwindling. It was unbearably humid inside and so dark that I had to use a flashlight to find my way up. Debris, dust, and cobwebs had piled up, blocking access to the remainder of the staircase. It had obviously been quite a while since someone had last trodden those stairs. In any event, technology took over a long time ago: the call to prayer now echoes effortlessly across the city via thousands of microphones that spare the callers the torture of ascending and descending endless stairs five times a day.

Domes, similarly, are not practical constructional solutions anymore. Quite the opposite: in comparison with flat concrete roofs or even cheap trusses, domes cost a fortune to build, and they take a long time to finish and decorate inside and out. But minarets and domes have long been more about symbolism than functionality. Today they denote Islamic pride and identity, which probably explains why many Muslims in Europe and elsewhere felt personally offended by the result of a referendum that banned building minarets in Switzerland.

Scene Six

If I were to list down all the funny, dreadful, and controversial stories I've heard in and about Friday sermons, I'd probably come up with a big fat book on that subject alone. (Mind you, it may not be such a bad idea after all. I might consider doing it one day.) Meanwhile, let me explain why those sermons made me quit praying at the mosque for several Fridays on end.

It wasn't until the early nineties that Friday sermons were broadcast live on the radio and on television from landmark mosques in Baghdad. It was a defining moment in Iraq's modern history: the political system was converting from strict secularism to right-wing Islamism. But long before Saddam's drastic turn in the nineties, President Anwar Sadat had decided to bring religion back to the Egyptians' daily lives, putting an end to the communism-oriented legacy of his predecessor, President Nasser. The stratagem was a big success at the time, and it had earned him massive popularity among the common people of Egypt. But it wasn't long before the pious leader had to reap what he'd sown. During a military parade in 1981, shortly after he had co-signed the Camp David peace accords with Israel, a group of fanatic Islamists assassinated him. Sadat had failed to see that religion was a double-edged sword that should have been handled with extreme caution.

Most Arabic channels today transmit Friday prayers live from either local mosques or the Sacred Mosque in Mecca. The call to prayer is broadcast five times a day, interrupting any program on national radio and television stations, with the exception of presidential or royal speeches. Almost all current Arab kings and presidents, some of whom claim descent from the Prophet, regularly appear on television praying at mosques while surrounded by their muscular bodyguards. They are keen to cultivate a public image of themselves as devout Muslims. It gives them legitimacy in the eyes of their people and implies unconditional obedience to their rule.

When I was a child, I took it for granted that every member of the clergy was wise and knowledgeable. I used to pay rapt attention to every word they'd utter in their Friday sermons, but after several consecutive disappointments, I gave up hope of finding decent ones. One day I noticed that I wasn't the only one in the mosque who'd lost interest in the sermon. When I looked around me, I saw people taking naps—despite the preacher's loud ranting. We were tired of hearing the same worn-out stories, and there was no question of probing any of the hard-core problems that burdened people: tyranny, poverty, corruption. Most imams resorted to the safety of repeating clichés for fear of losing their jobs—or their lives.

"Damn the music, singing, and dancing! Damn all sculptures and paintings! Damn the uncovered women! Damn the television and the Internet! Damn love, friendship, and any sort of illegitimate mixing between the sexes! Damn the homosexuals, damn the infidel Jews, the Christians, and the deviant Muslims of different sects! Damn democracy and may all disasters befall the depraved West! Damn the Americans, the British, and the Zionist Israelis, the children of apes and pigs! May they all burn to ashes in this life and then suffer eternal torment in the afterlife. But may God's blessings and protection be unto our leader. Amen!" Such was the type of rhetoric I had to endure during my Friday noon services until I couldn't stand the hypocrisy anymore.

Why must I go there to be showered with damns and curses? I asked myself time and again. *Don't we deserve any credit? Haven't we all come to pray and embrace the love of Allah? Why do we have to leave the mosque every week crippled by guilt and hatred?* I had to take a personal stance against what was happening. I knew my decision alone was not going to change a thing, but I had to make it for the sake of my self-esteem.-

Scene Seven

I've been told that in order to be permitted deliverance to the wide audience of worshippers, all sermons had to have several approvals in advance. Rumor also had it that many imams had secret ties to intelligence officials in the country. I don't know if it was true, but I had heard a number of them—especially the ones preaching at landmark mosques in Baghdad—shamelessly glorified Saddam on every possible occasion. A few, however, refused to conform, and dared to speak their minds. They were arrested on the spot and transported to prison camps. Many of them were never seen again.

Islamic imam-hood started as an honorary position given to the most religious among men to lead daily prayers at the mosque and deliver a guiding speech every Friday noon. Things have changed since then, and today's imams are solely selected and appointed by the Ministry for Islamic Affairs in each country. They are paid monthly salaries like all other public employees and are treated as such. But what does it take for a Muslim man to become a sheikh or an imam these days? First and foremost, applicants need to hold the equivalent to a bachelor's degree in Islamic studies from an accredited university or institute. A solid grounding in the areas of Islamic theology and Islamic history, Koran and Hadiths interpretations, Arabic literature, philosophy, logic, and psychology, as well as mastery of comparative religion must be acquired too. Sounds wonderful, but I only wish it were true!

I've heard imams inside Iraq and out make flagrant grammar mistakes not even elementary-school students would be allowed to make. Loaded with historical inaccuracies and a shameful lack of common sense and good structure, their sermons are both pointless and absurd. For some reason, all imams love to press the microphones right to their lips while they preach, and thanks to the invention of amplifiers, their high-pitched voices may be heard miles from their mosques. The whirlwind of noise at noon on Fridays makes it impossible for anyone in the city, let alone those living near mosques, to fall asleep, study, or even focus on anything until the entire service has ended, which may take as long as two hours.

Scene Eight

My shoes are gone! I waited until everybody had picked up his or her shoes, but mine had vanished.

"They must have been stolen," someone told me. "It's been happening every week during the past few months."

Every Friday, Muslims march in hundreds to their neighborhood mosques to perform the noon prayer. I've seen people blocking traffic on surrounding streets by spreading their prayer rugs on the pavement when indoor prayer halls were full. For an observant Muslim man, nothing, not rain or burning summer sun, should hinder him from praying at the mosque. Being a natural early bird, I always manage to find a decent place in the preferable front rows, but that too can have its share of disadvantages. The instant the service ends, people gather around the gates to collect their shoes. And beggars of all ages, tragic stories, and disabilities throng to seize the opportunity presented by post-prayer devotion. Those who pray outside have a better chance of keeping a close eye on their shoes, and put them on immediately after prayer, whereas early birds like myself have to line up for the shelves where we took our shoes off before entering the chapel. This is where unpleasant surprises are sometimes unavoidable.

Many Iraqis became destitute during the nineties. There had been a remarkable increase in the number of thefts and burglaries reported. It had never occurred to me until then that I could be robbed too. It's still hard to describe my feelings about it. Like all robbery victims, I was confused. But thinking that whoever it was that grabbed my shoes must have needed them desperately filled me with sadness and guilt.

Meanwhile, there was a technical problem to resolve. I didn't know what to do with my naked feet. It was quite a long walk to my house, and I couldn't ask people to lend me their shoes. I had no other alternative except to walk barefoot down to the street. While waiting for a taxi, I saw people smile at the sight of my feet, and when I finally reached home, opened the door, and walked in without my shoes, my family burst into hysterical laughter. I still remember that pair of Danish Eccos, probably because they were the only pistachio shoes I've ever had in my whole life. I never really liked the color, but it was sale season and the store had run out of blacks and browns. From the first time I tried them on at the store, they felt exceptionally comfortable. I'd already walked long miles in them when they were stolen. It's really sad to think people had become so poor that they had to steal a worn-out pair of green shoes from a shelf at the mosque while their owner was praying inside.

Scene Nine

On March 18th, 2005, a fifty-three-year-old woman in a loose Islamic robe with matching *hijab* stood before the rows of more than one hundred men and women to lead the Friday prayer in the Cathedral of St. John the Divine in New York. The proposal to host the ceremony had been rejected by several mosques in the city before finally settling on the church building. The woman-imam's name was Amina Wadud, an African-American professor of Islamic studies at Virginia Commonwealth University. She had converted to Islam when she was twenty. Amina gave a moving sermon to the small yet valiant audience unseparated by walls as in typical Islamic mosques. "With this prayer service we are moving forward," she told them. The next day, all hell broke loose!

I read about that incident, which made headlines around the world, in the newspapers. Professor Wadud's bold and brave initiative might not have been the first attempt to break the rigid, centuries-old traditions of prayer in Islamic mosques, but it definitely got the widest media coverage to date. Long years before that Friday in New York, I took my mother to attend the *Eid* prayer in our neighborhood mosque. She was so excited to go, and it was her first time visiting the place. We awoke early, performed ablutions, and left home before dawn had broken, although the service usually started twenty minutes after sunrise. I wanted to get there before all the streets were packed with cars. After I parked my car, my mother and I parted. I walked straight through the beautiful gate to the prayer hall, while she had to enter the mosque from a small side door that led to the women's quarters on the second floor.

The service was exceptionally good. Our imam preached compassion and tolerance, unlike the majority of imams who kept threatening people with the atrocities of hell, even in their holiday sermons. I left the mosque feeling refreshed and waited for my mother in the car. She showed up in a short while looking really upset.

"I'm not coming to this place anymore!" she said as she got into the car. "That women's chapel is awful. I had to climb the steep and narrow stairs to get there. It was totally dark, and I had to hold on tight to the wall until I finally made it to the smelly little room. I was barely able to kneel and prostrate. Many young mothers had brought along their children because their husbands wouldn't keep them. They kept jumping up and down, crying, and fighting with each other. I couldn't hear the imam's voice. Was it a good sermon?"

"It wasn't bad," I mumbled while guilt weighed heavily on me. I thought of the great time I just had and the celestial sensation of praying beneath the beautifully ornamented dome in the large prayer hall that smelled of fragrant incense, where I could see the imam and listen to every word he said. If God had equally commanded Muslim men and women to pray at exactly the same times of day and with exactly the same phrases and movements, why would He want them separated at the mosque? Where in the Koran did He ordain such segregation?

Men and women prayed in one chapel in the early mosques. The Prophet usually led the prayers, with the men lined behind him and the women right behind the men. I saw this happen at the Umayyad Mosque when I visited Damascus a few years ago: men and women prayed together inside the large rectangular prayer hall, separated only by barrier ropes. Also, Muslim men and women have been praying and circling the Ka'ba in Mecca shoulder to shoulder for the past fourteen centuries. There is no such thing as the women's quarters there. If the separation of the sexes does not apply at the Sacred Mosque in Mecca and did not apply at the first mosques during the Prophet's life, then why should it apply now?

In my search for the roots of segregation, I found some sayings of the Prophet that instructed Muslim women to pray in their homes instead of going to the mosque. I shall come back to this later on, but I need to point out here that several of Mohammed's alleged sayings are of ques- tionable authenticity. It's really hard to determine exactly which ones are true and which ones are not. Yet in extremely conservative communities, Muslim women are still being denied permission to leave their houses—not even to pray at the mosque—on no other basis than those controversial sayings of the Prophet. Surprisingly enough, some women don't seem to mind being treated this way. Polls in Saudi Arabia, for instance, have shown that the majority of Saudi women are against lifting the ban on women's driving in the country. The very idea of change frightens them, and they have reacted by refusing to step out of their comfort zone.

Ever since the early Muslims pledged themselves to spread the new canon to the world, Islam has been influenced by the civilizations it linked through conquest or commerce. The evolution of mosque architecture, as I've explained, is one good example of the ongoing interaction between the different cultures, but it's not the only one. With the noticeable growth rate of Islam around the world, new converts are still contributing to the tradition, reshaping it and adding to it.

On Sunday, March 7th, 2010, almost five years after Professor Wadud's maneuver, another American convert, Fatima Thompson, walked with a group of five women into the main prayer hall at the Islamic Center in Washington. Surprised and outraged, the imam immediately called the police, accusing the six intruders of disturbing prayer inside the mosque. "The general issue we are pushing is gender segregation and the ramifications it fosters. It's not healthy, and not reflective of our society here. It's very reflective of very restrictive, ultra-orthodox societies," Thompson told reporters. Several Arabic newspapers published the incident as delivered by AFP but most Muslim clerics kept silent. They had already expressed their resentment earlier and had nothing further to add.

More Inconveniences

Just before conducting prayer, the imam would usually turn around to address the gathering of men behind him, stressing the straightness of their lines. It is believed that Prophet Mohammed had frequently insisted that all the lines in prayer be perfectly straightened. Shoulder to shoulder and toe to toe, the men at the mosque have to make sure not to leave spaces between them, for gaps would invite the devil to penetrate their wall of faith. Connecting the lines also symbolizes unity amongst the believers, whereas uneven lines stand for dissension between the hearts. I personally have nothing against rules as long as they are reasonable. Order and discipline are vital to Islam as they are to any other religion. Only some Muslims tend to take things way too far!

One Friday noon, after the muezzin had finished giving the call to prayer and we were about to start praying, a young man with a big bushy beard from the back row inserted his large body between my neighbor and me. There were less than ten centimeters between us. I wouldn't call that a gap, but the young man decided to close it with his body. Prayer had already begun and it was too late to complain. Barely able to breathe with my ribcage squashed between my neighbors' arms, I had to hunch my shoulders to make room for his massive torso. I struggled even harder to prostrate my forehead to the floor, so angry that I couldn't wait for the prayer to end. The intruding young man left as soon as we finished, not caring one little bit about the disturbance he had caused. I encountered the same annoyance in different prayers at different mosques in different countries afterwards, and I still don't understand how causing so much discomfort to people while they pray is supposed to ward off the devil. In fact, I doubt that there could be a more appealing invitation!

Having to answer the call of nature in the middle of prayer at the mosque is another quandary. There is absolutely no dignified way to leave the prayer hall considering the high density of worshippers and their impenetrable lines. It is also prohibited to pass in front of a Muslim when he or she is praying. They would push the person back and force him to wait until prayer was over, ten or fifteen minutes at the most. People are allowed to move in and out during the sermon or the intervals between prayers. Ten minutes may not be such a long time for young and healthy worshippers, but it can mean a lot of suffering for people with certain ailments, the elderly, and children.

I once saw a little boy trying to leave the hall while we were praying on a Friday noon. He must have accompanied his father or one of his older brothers to the mosque, but everyone was praying, and they couldn't interrupt the ceremony to help him out. Spread arms blocked the poor child and cut him off in every direction he moved. He was so confused that his face turned red. Ashamed and helpless, he sat on the floor and burst into tears. It really broke my heart to see him weep like that, but I too couldn't do anything about it. No one was allowed to move, not even to give way to a little child to use the toilet.

Scene Ten

Abu Dhabi again. I had a few hours to spend in the airport on my way to Amman, Jordan, and I desperately needed to stretch my legs after more than fifteen hours of flying. As I sauntered through the aisles of the duty-free area, I had a sudden feeling that I was in a Southeast Asian airport. I found not one native Emirati among the many salesmen and saleswomen moving about the airport. All were Asians, which was the case in Doha International Airport too. I was starting to think it must be a regional thing in this rich part of the Arab world. Natives wouldn't enjoy being seen working!

I found a small bookstore with several magazine racks. The colorful photographs of movie stars and celebrities, both Arabs and Westerners, all over the glossy covers made me feel a bit dizzy. I turned to browse the books when a side shelf caught my attention. All the book covers carried a picture of an Arab-looking woman in a black veil, revealing dazzling eyes with vivid black lining against a background of domes and minarets. Right below the portrait I read, *A true story of honor killing*. And on another book: *A true story of a Muslim woman's struggle for freedom*, for love, et cetera, et cetera. I had barely finished writing a few pages about Muslim women, and there I was worrying about my prospective book's cover, fearing it could end up looking like those *true story* books on the shelf in front of me. *What nonsense! It must be my jet lag.* I really needed to have some coffee.

My back was aching badly, and the last thing I wanted

to do was sit down again. I sipped my coffee standing up and saw a mosque sign. I thought it might be a good idea to make a short prayer. I needed to move my body anyway. I followed the arrows, *et voila*, I was there. A small room with bare walls and modest carpeting. *Perfect,* I thought, *I couldn't ask for more.* The usual ornaments would have only increased my dizziness.

The soothing effect of cold water while performing my ablutions was so intense it made me linger in the washroom for a while. I then grabbed some tissues to dry my face and walked barefoot to the small chapel. I put my laptop case and trolley bag aside and started praying. Dawn prayer had already finished when I arrived, so I had to pray solo, which I really didn't mind; it's the shortest of the five daily prayers, so it only took me a few minutes to finish. I picked one of the several Korans on the shelf and started reading; then I noticed there was another man in the room.

He was still praying when I finished reading. I put the Koran back on the shelf and sat on the floor, resting my back against the wall for a few minutes before resuming my trip. This middle-aged Caucasian man kept on praying as if I didn't exist. His eyes were closed while a ghost of a smile lit up his face. He was whispering the verses to himself. I wondered if he could understand Arabic, but he didn't seem to have a problem with it. I'd seen thousands of people pray before but this time it was different.

This man is beaming with contentment, I thought. Although his body was there in the room, his soul seemed to have taken off with some sacred communion. I had seen the trancelike expression before on the faces of Turkish Sufi Dervishes as they performed their *Sama*: right palms pointing to the sky, left palms towards the earth, and their bodies whirling faster and faster, counter-clockwise. They seemed disconnected from our worldly life. I watched them dance and wondered about the mystical journey their souls were embarking upon. Their sweaty faces looked peaceful and serene just like the face of the praying middle-aged Caucasian man in front of me.

As he prostrated, I picked up my luggage and left the place. I didn't want him to open his eyes and find me staring at him, and it was time to catch my next flight anyway. I put my shoes on and walked hurriedly towards my gate, but I could not forget the way he had been praying. In the small mosque with bare walls and modest carpeting at Abu Dhabi International Airport, not very far from one of the largest and most luxurious mosques in the world, I had observed a revelation. That man had captured the very essence of his being, and it radiated into me.

CHAPTER 8

Try a Free Sample of Religion!

CALL UNTO THE PATH OF YOUR LORD WITH
WISDOM AND GOOD PREACHING, AND BRING
THEM TO REASON IN THE MOST TEMPERATE
MANNER, FOR YOUR LORD KNOWS BEST
THOSE WHO HAVE STRAYED FROM HIS PATH,
AS HE KNOWS THE GUIDED ONES.

(16.125)

"Non-Muslims are prohibited from attending Al-Azhar University." I was surprised when I first read the statement on the Annual Report, issued by the United States Commission on International Religious Freedom. I found that utterly discriminatory and incomprehensible, given the university's core mission of propagating the Islamic faith throughout the world. When I asked my Egyptian friend Ali about the matter, he confirmed: indeed, Al-Azhar University—the world's oldest and probably most acclaimed Islamic university—does not admit non-Muslim students, not even to its secular faculties of medicine, engineering, business, and other sciences. My memory reverted back to my school years in Baghdad.

Scene One

American Jesuit priests established Baghdad College, a once-elite high school for boys, in 1931. Within a few years of its foundation, the institute had become a favored destination for Baghdadi students from well-off families despite a latent suspicion in the conservative Muslim community about its purpose. After the school's first alumni had proven themselves so highly qualified that many were admitted to prestigious universities in the United Kingdom and the United States, all fears subsided and the school earned a reputation for being Iraq's best high school for boys. By the time I was enrolled, Baghdad College—as well as the other private schools—had long been nationalized. Shortly after the Ba'athist coup d'état in 1968, the government decided to take full control of the school, and the Jesuit teachers were given only a few days to leave the country. Today, other than the small crosses along the roof balustrades of its buildings and the church annexed to it, there is hardly any trace left of the school's missionary years.

Spread over a vast area, the school's main three buildings were constructed in a typical British Colonial style. Large football fields and basketball, handball, and tennis courts surround them. The school kept its special English-teaching program, its well-equipped library, and its science laboratories and was, therefore, still in high demand. I had to pass oral and written tests before I was finally admitted. As it happened, Saddam's sons Uday and Qusay were among the school's students at the time. While Uday was a loud exhibitionist, Qusay was rather quiet and circumspect. But the dangerous presidential brothers were both older than I, so I only saw them during lunch breaks, and—abiding by my parents' advice—I always made sure to keep my distance.

For more than eighty years, Baghdad College and other missionary schools have graduated tens of thousands of Muslim students, many of whom have become prominent scholars, politicians, scientists, businessmen, and artists. I don't remember hearing about any conversions among the school's alumni. Actually, quite a considerable number of my old school friends are now strictly observant Muslims. They pray, fast, give alms, and don't drink alcohol or eat pork. If anything, I think that our time in Baghdad College helped us become more understanding and accepting of the other religions, Christianity in particular.

Scene Two

I believe Christian missionaries of almost every existing church have targeted me in every imaginable way since I left Iraq:

- Fervent young men chasing me down the street of my New Zealand neighborhood, offering to visit me and my family to talk about the love of Jesus Christ;
- Elderly Jehovah's Witnesses paying their unsolicited visits or just dropping their leaflets through my door;
- Taxi drivers wearing beatific smiles while telling me how the Gospel rescued them from addiction;
- Undisclosed Catholics sending me emails that

viciously attack the Prophet and ridicule every single aspect of Islam.

There are also the Christian shows on television I occasionally stumble upon while channel-surfing on my couch at night. As an Arab Muslim, I really don't mind all this. I mean, as long as they are not overly pushy or disrespectful, I see no reason why I should decline or avoid them.

Based on my personal experience, I can say there are two basic, yet very different schools of evangelism. The one I prefer is that which does not offend other people's faiths, but rather focuses on demonstrating the goodness of its own doctrine. I try to look at it this way: imagine your new neighbors invite you for dinner at their place one night. From the moment you walk through their door, you are inspired. Everything seems to fit together perfectly. Afterward, you go home and move a couch in your living room, hang a painting on your wall, or install a new lampshade. Some missionaries are gifted with the ability to inspire others in this way. I love to be inspired, and I seek inspiration all the time. But inspiration doesn't necessarily lead to conversion. In fact, it sometimes enhances one's original faith.

Scene Three

Iraq, like Lebanon, is a unique mosaic of ethnicities and faiths: Arabs, Kurds, Turkmen, Persians, Armenians, Shia Muslims, Sunni Muslims, Chaldean Christians, Syriacs, Assyrians, Jews, Mandaeans, Yazidis, Baha'is, and others have all lived there for centuries. Of course, there have been several conflicts along the way, but never in our modern history have relations between fellow Iraqis been as tense as they are now. It wasn't until I was fourteen that I knew about the Shia and the Sunnis and learned that my brothers and I were the children of a mixed marriage. I had many friends just like us, and people didn't pay much attention to these things back then. The war in 2003 was a pivotal event: all of a sudden, it emerged that there was nothing more important in life than religious identity. Violence and rancor broke out.

What started as a cheerful reunion of good old friends soon transformed into an unpleasant, unfriendly feud. I found myself caught in the middle of an obnoxious debate over which Islamic sect was right and which was wrong. Being the son of a mixed marriage between a Shia man and a Sunni woman, I kept silent while my friends passionately disputed their beliefs. My Sunni friend told a joke about the Shia rituals. My Shia friend didn't laugh. My Sunni friend then criticized the Shias' historical attachment to Persia and their self-flagellation over the massacre of the saints that had taken place long centuries ago. Even though much of my Sunni friend's criticism was valid, little did it matter to my Shia friend because he was no longer listening. I saw his face turn red with anger. He retorted with a long list of charges against the Sunnis: bigotry, hostility, even terrorism. When we left the coffee shop that night, the once-close childhood friends shook hands coldly and would probably never meet again.

There are no winners in religious debates, even though

all adversaries would like to think they have defeated their foes. Truth is, they only have been fighting in vain. I imagine my Shia friend drawing back his early childhood memories. The fragrance of incense, the way the solemn rhythm of drumbeats made his heart pound, the taste of the food his mother was cooking, and the safety he felt when she took him in her warm arms. How could he possibly betray his mother's memory by conceding that our Sunni friend might have a point?

Many missionaries fail to see the futility of religious debates. Like vicious warriors, they use all their weapons to attack your faith and would spend long hours pushing you to adopt theirs. Most of the time, they get turned down, if not attacked back because they have missed the main point: a person's religion, good or bad—although I don't think there is such a thing as an *all-good* or *all-bad* religion—becomes a basic feature of his or her identity over the years. Attempting to disentangle people from their religion, unless they are responding to an inner calling, is an almost hopeless mission.

Scene Four

So now we have the good guys and the bad guys, but is that all? No, there are subdivisions too. At the end of the day, missionaries (and politicians) are like street vendors: they need to attract and encourage people to buy their goods, and for that purpose, they use different tactics, both legal and illegal. In extremely poor countries, the destitute may sell their votes to the highest bidders among candidates. It happens often and is sometimes considered normal. Like desperate prostitutes, they are willing to do everything and anything to feed their children, even if it costs them feigning a spiritual orgasm.

Immediately after the American invasion, several Iraqi cities, especially in the north, witnessed a flood of American missionaries. I'd read about it in several newspapers, although I hadn't seen any of them in Baghdad, probably because they had set the poor rural towns and villages as their target markets. They arrived loaded with generous humanitarian aid and of course Gospel parables. It is said that a drowning man will clutch at a straw, and this was exactly what some Iraqis did in order to survive. They pretended to have converted to Christianity, and with the help of the missionaries in their villages, they fled to Europe or the United States to claim asylum based on religious persecution. Once admitted, local Christian organizations would help them settle into life. Many of them used the money they received to support their poor families in Iraq. Deception was their only way to ensure a safe and decent future for themselves and their children, and it would be unfair to blame them for that.

Scene Five

Coercion, bribery, and persuasion. The history of Islam exemplifies almost all schools of spreading religion. I remember when I was a youngster in Baghdad, one of my history teachers took great pride in describing the Muslim conquerors in Europe, Asia, and Africa as glorious liberators, the same way some right-wing American politicians today describe the invasion and occupation of Iraq as liberation. But I guess it's a common thing to have diverse interpretations and even misconceptions like this because our reading of history has always been and will always be subjective.

Many historians would agree, though, that the Muslims' rule in Spain was a time of religious and ethnic tolerance, during which architecture, science, philosophy, literature, and the arts all prospered. At the same time, there is no denying that the native Spanish, Christians, and Jews were forced to choose between converting to Islam and paying *jizya*, a tax imposed on non-Muslim subjects alone. Several cathedrals were also demolished, and others were converted into mosques. Almost eight centuries later, Spain saw history repeat itself when Granada, the last Islamic citadel in Andalusia, surrendered to the new Catholic monarchs Ferdinand and Isabella. Before long, all mosques were turned to churches, and the Muslim population had to either convert to Roman Catholicism or return to their ancestral lands.

By the time Granada fell into the hands of the Spanish, a few good Muslim merchants were making a big difference at the other end of the world. Over two hundred million Muslims make Indonesia today the world's most populous Muslim country. Many Indonesians are Arabic-illiterate, yet they are consistent in memorizing the verses of the Koran in Arabic through repetitive recitation. They pray five times a day, fast the whole month of Ramadan, give alms, and undertake the pilgrimage to Mecca. They may very well be more observant than many contemporary Arab Muslims, including myself.

The ancient Muslim traders unwittingly introduced their faith to the Malay Peninsula and the islands of the Indonesian archipelago by impressing their partners with their honesty and straightforwardness. The rulers of the lands voluntarily converted to Islam from Buddhism and Hinduism, and the common people soon followed their lead. In just a few centuries, the new religion took over vast areas of Southeast Asia and has prevailed there ever since.

Scene Six

I have to admit that I'm often jealous of the fine reputation missionary Christian schools, hospitals, and other institutions enjoy throughout the Arab world. Among the best-reputed universities in the Arab world today are the American University of Beirut—founded in 1862 by American Protestant missionaries in Syria and Lebanon— and the American University in Cairo, 1919. But they are not the only ones. Several American universities have been and will be opening their doors to Arab students, Muslims and non-Muslims alike, in Dubai, Sharjah, Kuwait, Madaba in Jordan, and even Iraqi Kurdistan. Catholic missionaries, on the other hand, have been exceptionally skillful at running schools and hospitals. St. Raphael's Hospital is one of the best, if not the best, in Baghdad. The hospital, as well as a girls' school, have been run by the Dominican Sisters of St. Catherine of Siena, a Catholic community founded in Iraq at the end of the nineteenth century.

Why does everything efficient, disciplined, and clean have to be run by some Christian church? I'm clueless. Some folks would say this is all part of their missionary work— that is, to create a good impression of their churches. And in order to achieve that, they receive generous donations from devout Christians around the world. But if the native Muslims are not converting to Christianity, what use is it for Western churches to spend so much effort and money running hospitals, rest homes, orphanages, and schools overseas?

The early missionaries to the region were well aware of the near-impossibility of attracting Muslims to convert to Christianity. Instead, they aimed at converting the native Christians of the Orthodox Eastern church into Catholicism and, later, Protestantism. And indeed, they succeeded in inspiring and converting many. This strategy, later on, was modified to include Muslims as well. "Christian efforts have found Islamic regions to be very resistant. I would not expect that in the Islamic world there's going to be any immediate receptivity to organized Christian efforts. I think this situation calls for great wisdom and responsibility on the part of Christian organizations, as well as a full measure of conviction," said Albert Mohler, the president of the Southern Baptist Theological Seminary, to Broward Liston in an interview for *Time Magazine* shortly after the war in Iraq, 2003.

Scene Seven

Muslim and Christian evangelists may be scuffling over

winning new converts to their faiths, but I have to admit that out of the three Abrahamic religions, we Muslims are the most paranoid when it comes to being subjected to missionary activities. Our inner alarm bells scream whenever others approach us. But if Islam is a solid faith that stands on its own merits, and I believe it is, then why do we fear rivalry and challenge so much?

In fact, the West hasn't always been this tolerant and accepting of other religions. We all know what the Nazis did to millions of European Jews during World War II, although some would argue that the Holocaust wasn't really a religious genocide so much as an ethnic or cultural one. Still, it's hard to deny that there was at least some kind of religious background to it. But either way, things have changed. Most Western societies have turned to secularism; freedom of religion, including the freedom of practicing and propagating faith, is constitutionally guaranteed. The constitutions of several Arab countries do recognize freedom of religion as a fundamental right for every citizen, but as often happens with constitutional rights in the Arab world, freedoms are easily breached and suppressed.

It is a natural inclination for human beings to share their beliefs with others. After all, we are social creatures. Muslims love to call other people to our religion, but when it's the other way around, when others try to teach us about their faiths, we get agitated. Foreign missionaries are rarely, if ever, welcome in our countries. They only do their work in secret, and if they are caught, they are usually deported immediately. This attitude, I'm afraid, delivers the wrong message to the world. Only the weak are afraid of competition.

In our capitalistic world, even missionaries need to master the art of marketing to get their work done. Good quality may impress buyers, but whether we like it or not, without having a creative marketing plan, it's really hard to sell anything these days. Many manufacturers offer free samples of their products to consumers in the supermarkets and at homes. If the sample is good and competitive, people will adopt it; if not, they will throw it away. There is no place anymore for force or coercion. Everything should be done in an attractive, smooth, and subtle way. It may be time for Muslims to learn to accept competition as part of contemporary life.

CHAPTER 9

No Halal Bacon on Board

O YOU WHO HAVE BELIEVED, FORBID NOT
THE GOOD THINGS WHICH GOD HAS MADE
LAWFUL FOR YOU, BUT TRANSGRESS NOT, FOR
GOD ABHORS TRANSGRESSORS. AND EAT OF
THAT WHICH GOD HAS PROVIDED FOR YOU,
LAWFUL AND GOOD, AND REVERE GOD, IN
WHOM YOU BELIEVE.

(5.87,88)

H*alal* in Arabic means *lawful and permitted by God.*
Its antonym *haram* means unlawful and forbidden,
with a few exceptions. The Sacred Mosque in Mecca, for
instance, is called *Al Masjid Al Haram* for no profanity or
fighting is allowed in any form whatsoever there. Likewise,
certain months in the Islamic lunar calendar are called
the *Haram* Months. Nowadays, *halal* and *haram* are probably among the most commonly used words in our Islamic
conversations.

Scene One

Summer 1955: Among the 2300 passengers on board the ocean liner RMS *Queen Elizabeth* that had just left Southampton in England on its way to New York City, there was a young physician on his first ocean cruise. Or, to be more precise, his first-ever trip outside of his homeland, Iraq. He woke up early the first morning at sea, pulled himself out of his narrow bed, got dressed, and quickly looked at himself in the small mirror on the wall while combing his hair with Brylcreem. His hair was noticeably thinning, but he still had a fair amount of it left—the family's baldness gene so strong that it would pass to his yet-to-be-born two sons. Done with the hair, he then walked to the large dining room to have his first breakfast on board after a long night of frequent, seasickness-induced vomiting.

Driven by his medical awareness that his body needed fluids and protein in order to survive, he forced himself to eat. He wanted to feel better so that he could explore the famous ship he had hardly gotten any chance to see the night before. As you might have guessed by now, the young Iraqi physician going to the United States of America in pursuit of his postgraduate degree in Internal Medicine was my father.

Before he could touch the scrambled eggs and the crispy slices of fried meat on the plate, a young man approached him out of the blue, asking, "Are you a Muslim?" My father, not grasping what religion had to do with having breakfast, answered, "Yes, I am."

"Are you aware of what you're about to eat?" Before

my father even had the chance to answer what seemed like a riddle, the stranger went on: "I'm a physician from Yugoslavia, and I'm a Muslim too. Be careful! This is bacon—it's pig meat."

As if my father's stomach needed that! He managed to drink a little tea and went straight to bed, where he would spend most of the following days and nights until the big boat finally reached its destination. There was nothing more cheerful to him than the sight of seagulls and the Statue of Liberty on the horizon. Almost all of the passengers had gathered on deck.

"Sir, do you know who is the voice of America?" a drunk man jokingly asked my father, who must have been so weak that he lacked the energy to smile, let alone answer. The drunken man said, "It's Marilyn Monroe!"

Several years after docking at the land of big dreams, my father, having finished his studies, decided to go back to Iraq. He got married and had three children, a girl and two boys. I'm the youngest.

I've heard this story time and again and thought it was quite interesting. I guess all kids like adventure stories, and exploring a new continent on a multi-storey boat that has sailed the wild ocean was just perfect for me. I remembered the drunken man's joke when I opened the door one day in 2003 and saw an American tank right in front of our house. I was taken aback. The soldier up there waved his hand at me. I nodded my head, turned around, and locked the door again. I wonder who the voice of America is today.

Scene Two

We were taught in school that God didn't want us to consume pork because it's dirty meat. It had worms that could cause severe, incurable illness, and because God loved us Muslims so much, He had commanded us not to eat it. I don't know whose idea it was to engrain such a premise into our little minds. Yes, in the Koran God does forbid us from eating pork, but there is no explanation as to why He doesn't want us to eat it. He just doesn't! The worms trick, nevertheless, worked like magic. We all grew up loathing pork.

But is pork really bad? I have found many allegations online, and several Islamic websites even mention the old worms story. Although they all claim pork is detrimental to health and a very bad source of protein compared to other types of meat, I haven't found any credible scientific research supporting that. Most doctors agree that pork, like any other meat or food, is safe for human consumption as long as it's eaten in moderation and is handled and cooked properly. This is quite interesting because I've often thought that if pork were so dangerous, then how come people who have never touched it—practicing Muslims and Jews—aren't healthier than those who have? We don't live longer than people who eat pork, and we don't show signs of intellectual superiority over them. Both groups share the same list of diseases: cancer, Alzheimer's, depression, diabetes, and hypertension. And by itself, skipping pork seems to give neither Muslims nor Jews any special protection against infection. Not even against flu.

Fornication, negligence of prayer, lying, arrogance, envy,

and gossip are as sinful as pork-eating in God's sight. Some sins like murder, theft, and adultery are considered much worse, yet some people can't totally avoid them the way they can avoid eating pig meat. Why? Because there are no *halal* alternatives. Take, for example, sex and our natural need for it. Fewer and fewer young men and women are able to marry because of soaring poverty and unemployment. But they, or some of them, can't live without sex. Our bodies keep asking for it, and in the absence of lawful fulfillment of our natural needs, committing *haram* may be inevitable.

Abstaining from pork, however, is an easy, if not the easiest, commitment for a Muslim to carry out. It gives us the contentment and pride of having obeyed God's commands at almost no cost, effort, or suffering. Only a few shops and supermarkets sell pork to foreigners or native Christians, most of whom only eat it occasionally, if ever. Unlike rice, bread, beef, chicken, or lamb, pork is not an integral part of our traditional food system, so we don't miss it when it's gone. We don't even know what it tastes like. I've heard bacon is salty and fatty, but so what? Processed meats nowadays offer lots of *halal* choices for Muslim consumers. Turkey and chicken bacons are available in many Islamic countries, and they taste exactly like the original pork bacon, or so I have been told.

Scene Three

The rules with regard to food and drink had not changed much since my father's trip to the United States in the fifties until the nineties when I visited Thailand. Everything was permitted except pork and alcohol. In my father's case, he could only refrain from the former, but not the latter. He started drinking while he was at university in Baghdad, and it grew even worse when he went to the States. However, after surviving a myocardial infarction in the mid-seventies, he quit drinking and smoking. That was probably the bravest decision of his life.

On our visit to London in 1981, I was told I was free to eat everything I wanted unless the food was clearly pork, bacon, or ham. And by *clearly* I mean these ingredients had to be specified in the menu. I was only twelve then, and I would innocently walk into a nearby pizzeria and pick toppings like pepperoni and salami, thinking they were all *halal*. I also remember when we visited Vienna, Frankfurt, and Munich, my father would often buy us huge sausage sandwiches with lots of mustard sauce. We loved the sandwiches; they were so delicious. Only I'm not sure if my father bothered to ask about the meat beforehand. But even if he had, I guess it wouldn't have made much difference given that most people there could barely speak English.

There are, nevertheless, very few exceptions to the ban on eating pork. In cases of absolute necessity, if a Muslim got lost in the desert and had to choose between dying of hunger and eating pork—assuming pork was available in the desert at that moment—he or she may eat it in order to survive. It is not a sin either if a Muslim were to eat pork unsuspectingly or by mistake. This means I don't need to beat myself up over my pepperoni pizza in London or my German frankfurters: I didn't know they had pork in them.

Even so, all Muslims should be careful about what they put in their mouths. I try to do that now, but not obsessively.

Shortly after our London trip, traveling abroad was banned for all Iraqis. The war with Iran was consuming much of the country's resources, hardly leaving any margin for vanities like tourism. The combat between the two Muslim neighbors ended after eight long years, and in 1990 I set out on my first trip as an adult, to Thailand, where I made sure not to miss out on a single pleasure. I ate everywhere in Bangkok and savored all the delights that came my way: Thai, Chinese, Indian, Italian, even junk food—I spared nothing. Again, unless pork was clearly mentioned, or the meal served seemed suspiciously pinkish or purplish, all was *halal* to me.

That trip, however, was exceptional in more than one way. I remember when the Iraqi Airways Boeing landed in Baghdad International Airport, the airport staff was acting strangely. Everyone seemed disturbed and confused. I had no idea what was going on. I came back on August 2, 1990, immediately after the Iraqi army had invaded Kuwait. It turned out that our plane was the last to land before the airport was closed. Another war would break out in a few months. Only this time, it was much more vicious than the one that had just ended.

It didn't take the coalition of more than thirty countries led by the United States long to force the Iraqi army out of Kuwait. But the First Gulf War—as it came to be known—left unprecedented destruction throughout Iraq. Life became unbearable for many Iraqis, and thousands of young men and women decided to leave. Only a few Arab countries like Jordan, Yemen, and Libya let them in. Traveling to the West was out of the question: no Western country agreed to give us visas during that time. Of course, in Arab or Muslim countries there is no need to check for *halal* labels in the supermarkets or on restaurants' menus. But this was certainly not the case in the European and American cities that accepted groups of Iraqi refugees after the Second Gulf War in 2003. Also, a new definition of *halal* had emerged. It was no longer confined to the avoidance of pork and alcohol.

Scene Four

The new criteria stated that no meat was *halal*—except fish—unless slaughtered and produced in accordance with Sharia standards. This means poultry, beef, and lamb all have to be purchased from either certified *halal* or kosher stores. Otherwise, they are not lawful for Muslim consumption. But how is *halal* chicken or kosher chicken different from any other chicken? The answer to my naïve question, it turns out, involves several technical and religious factors, many of which I'm not knowledgeable enough to discuss here. But let me try to put it in a nutshell: both *halal* and kosher slaughter share similar rituals. They slit the throat of the animal with a very sharp knife to reduce pain, and they let all the blood drain from the carcass before proceeding with cutting the parts. In *halal* abattoirs, however, God's name should be pronounced during the process as well.

Animal welfare groups in the West criticize the

throat-slitting method for cruelty. It has been replaced in many parts of the world with a new technique that uses stunning the animals with electrodes, or drowning birds in scalding water, or just wringing their necks before slaughter. While it is still disputable which method is more humane and less painful to the animals, there is an enormous demand for *halal* meat from hundreds of millions of Muslims around the world, a huge market estimated at more than five hundred billion American dollars a year.

But why now? Why not decades or even centuries earlier, when all Muslims had to avoid was pork and alcohol? I dare to ask another naïve question, but I seriously don't understand. If the new slaughter rules are derived from the Koran, as many scholars would insist, and given that the Koran has been around for many centuries now, then why have the new restrictions only emerged during the past decade or two? I tried to get an answer from the many Islamic sites on the Internet. As usual, I ended up with lots of different, sometimes contradictory, opinions.

The puritan Sheikhs say there has hardly been any change. *Halal* definition and rules are much the same as ever. God gives Muslims permission to eat the food of the People of the Book—Christians and Jews—as long as it meets the basic Sharia standards. First, it has to be free of pork and alcohol. And second, the animal must be alive, healthy, and conscious at the moment its neck is cut. This last requirement is no longer being met at many Western slaughterhouses, which makes their food unlawful for Muslims.

The constraints don't stop here. The ban has been extended to include all food products and even medications and cosmetics that contain animal-derived ingredients like gelatin. Everything should be *halal*-tested and certified. Some extremists would argue that even if the Western slaughterhouses and factories followed the Islamic guidelines, their products would still be non-*halal* because they employ non-Muslim workers. In brief, what used to be the easiest of commitments is not so easy anymore. All Muslims living abroad, and I'm no exception, cannot have a beef burger or fried chicken at Western restaurants and think that just by skipping pork they are keeping a clear conscience towards their religion. Worse yet, we are expected to avoid all the places that serve non-*halal* meals and should not even have a green salad there for fear of contaminated utensils. I have even received emails calling for a ban on all cola drinks because they contain an enzyme extracted from pig intestines, and another to boycott all food products that use additives known as the E Numbers for the same reason. (This may be a great tip for healthy eating because it's really hard to think of any processed food that doesn't have them.)

A family friend unloaded when I asked for his opinion on the *halal* and non-*halal* controversy: "When people ask me, I tell them I only buy *halal* meat from the Islamic butchery. To be honest, I used to do that until I realized the meat there wasn't as fresh as the non-*halal* chicken, beef, and lamb I bought from the supermarket. We have to be practical. We're living in a Western country. When you're invited to a barbecue, it's kind of crazy to pass up the scrumptious beefsteaks just because the meat is non-*halal*. It's not like we are eating pork or drinking wine, God forbid!"

If the *halal* regulations and restrictions keep getting tighter and tighter, I'm not sure if they can still be maintained in a modern-day lifestyle.

Scene Five

In 2006, I traveled to Malaysia, a beautiful country with a Malay Muslim majority as well as a considerable Chinese and Indian population. Islam is the official religion of the federation, and just like in all Arab countries, *halal* food is everywhere, even in fast-food outlets like McDonald's and Burger King. The places that sell and serve non-*halal* meat, nevertheless, have to put up signs declaring it in order to avoid any possible confusion.

I was window-shopping one day in one of Kuala Lumpur's massive malls when a sign posted on a shoe shop completely took me by surprise: *We sell* halal *leather shoes.*

Why should I care if my shoes are *halal* or not? What difference would that make? I'm not going to eat them! Is there even such a thing as *halal* shoes? I thought that was ridiculous, and I still do. But it was on that trip that I first realized how much *halal*'s definition has expanded.

Scene Six

Each time I talk to an old friend on the phone or online, we reminisce about our good old days in Baghdad. Strangely enough, even when we recall our memories of war now, we somehow manage to find moments of happiness in them: a joke someone had cracked during bombardment; a heated game of Monopoly, Risk, or Cluedo; or simply a walk in winter sun with friends when schools and universities were closed. Whenever I ask my friends now about a childhood, high school, or university friend, I'm told he or she is living somewhere outside Iraq. Some are residing in neighboring countries like Jordan or Syria, while others are working in the rich states of the Gulf. But the majority have settled and earned citizenship in Europe, Australia, Canada, and the United States. There are no accurate statistical data on this matter, although in 2007, the UN Refugee Agency estimates the number of Iraqis displaced by violence after the last war alone to be more than four million—more than half of whom fled the country to live abroad as refugees.

While it may still be possible for the Muslims living in major Western cities to find *halal* food and restaurants at reasonably affordable prices, it's quite a dilemma for those living in the suburban or rural areas, especially if they have school-age children, as many Muslim families do. Try to imagine how a little child would feel when his parents deprive him of chocolates, cakes, marshmallows, and ice cream while grocery-shopping in the supermarket or walking through the malls. He sees all the mouth-watering food he's been watching other children excitedly devour, but he's not allowed to touch it. And he doesn't even know why.

The systematic suppression of Muslim children's desires makes them feel they're being punished for reasons unknown to them, and will eventually lead them to create a secret world of sinful fantasies, where everything pretty, joyful, and delicious is kept hidden. This alternative world is much more beautiful than the dull and austere lawful world of their parents, but they can't forsake either one. The former gives them happiness, and the latter gives them communal acceptance and protection, and they need both, so they split in two. The children of fanatic Muslim families in the West often end up being disliked and rejected by their classmates in school. From day one, their parents strictly warn them not to share meals or hang out with their infidel peers.

Sooner or later there comes a time when a son or a daughter can't take their parents' pressure any longer, and why should they? They leave the obnoxious prison walls behind to practice their lawful freedoms elsewhere. Their parents watch them go astray and can't do a thing to stop them. Well, some of them can. Every now and then Muslim fathers in the West make headlines for shooting dead a young daughter who refused to cover her hair, or a son who converted to another religion or even became an atheist. Thankfully, in the case of food, the extremist interpretation of the *halal* verses in the Koran is not the only one we have.

A number of liberal scholars, not many though, have given permission to the Muslims living in non-Muslim countries to eat all food except pork. Many Muslims I know believe that mentioning the name of God before eating makes food safe and lawful. I heard my sister telling this to her friend—a recently admitted immigrant to Canada. This civil engineer and mother of three children who wore *hijab* and observed daily prayers sounded exasperated on the phone: "This is unbearable. These clergy have gone absolutely mad. Their obsession with *halal* and non-*halal* has gone way beyond reason. What on Earth is left for us and our children to eat with all these stupid bans?"

Scene Seven

God doesn't mind us asking for concessions, for He knows our frailty well. I developed this conviction after I read about the Prophet's Night Journey. The Koran doesn't give much detail about the occurrence, yet it mentions that Mohammed, while sleeping at night, was taken on a journey to Jerusalem, where the Dome of the Rock Mosque would be built almost seven decades later. And from there, he headed heavenwards. We don't know whether the Prophet traveled with his physical body or whether it was only his soul that transcended the material world to come closer to the Source of Light than any other human being had ever been allowed to. Bearing in mind that many of these stories could not be fully trusted, I tried to learn more about the journey from the early narratives of the Prophet's companions who transmitted his account of the experience.

What I found most interesting in the books I read on Mohammed's Night Journey was the story of his meeting with the previous messengers. God had first prescribed fifty prayers a day for every Muslim, but had this reduced to only five after the Prophet talked with Moses—who was by that time experienced in dealing with rebellion against God's laws. Moses advised Mohammed to go back to God and suggest a reduction. Mohammed took Moses' advice and kept negotiating until the fifty prayers became five. It is even narrated in some books that Moses encouraged the Prophet to push a little harder, but he did not. He was too embarrassed to bargain with God any further.

Like many other religious stories, there is absolutely no way of finding out if this one is true or merely allegorical. The way I look at it, it offers a valuable opportunity for understanding God and the way He viewed our human imperfections. Its meaning goes beyond the number of prescribed daily prayers (although, to be honest, there are times when I wish the negotiations could have proceeded a little bit more!) by showing us that God is approachable. He is not a heartless banker who will confiscate your property if you fail to pay your debts on time.

This conceptualization helps me tackle the many issues related to *halal* and *haram*, lawful and unlawful, in my daily life. If it were left up to the clerics, they would never cease complicating our lives in the name of religion. This is their job; it feeds them and their families. The greater the confusion, the more people will run to them for answers. I know I will not eat pork even if it is proven to be the healthiest meat to consume. Abstinence has become a part of me I neither can nor want to give up. But it's much bigger than food; it's about building a personal mechanism for coping with religious restrictions wherever and whenever they arise. And they so often do.

CHAPTER 10

Into the Garden

THOSE WHO HAVE BELIEVED AND THE JEWS
AND THE CHRISTIANS AND THE SABIANS,
WHOEVER BELIEVED IN GOD AND THE LAST
DAY AND DID RIGHTEOUS ACTS SHALL HAVE
THEIR REWARD FROM THEIR LORD, AND NO
FEAR SHALL BE UPON THEM NOR SHALL THEY
EVER GRIEVE.

(2.62)

From the moment I first realized there were people in this world who were not Muslims, until the day I started looking at myself, the others, and God in a different light, it has been a long journey.

Scene One

"I will pray to God to bless and look after you and your family in Baghdad," my American friend Christine said after we'd had a good chat online about politics. She wanted to know more about the situation in Iraq after the war and whether life had become any better after Saddam.

"Thanks, Christine. That is so nice of you. I too shall pray for you and your family in the States," I said, overwhelmed by the kindness of her gesture.

In Iraq, somehow, we always managed to differentiate between the American people and the American politicians who have been sabotaging our country, or what was left of it, during the past few decades. In the days that followed the war in 2003, some Iraqis went as far as serving the American soldiers in their neighborhoods food and tea as a token of amity. These sentiments, however, were soon to change as people's hopes of a peaceful and prosperous future started to evaporate.

"No, please don't!" Christine's line came out of nowhere and caught me off guard.

Certain there must have been some misunderstanding, I asked, "Why not?"

"Please don't take it personally. It's not about you. I totally understand your good intentions and I thank you for them. It's just that I cannot accept your praying to a deity other than Jesus Christ for me." This devout Catholic girl, pursuing higher studies in mechanical engineering at a prestigious university, was freaked out at the prospect of a Muslim man praying for her to *his* God not *hers*! I stared at the computer screen, baffled and not getting what was going on. Was she serious?

Scene Two

All three of us lived in the same neighborhood and went to the same high school. My friends Raad and Imad were two years my senior, though. Raad is a religious Muslim. His father, a renowned lawyer, provided his family with a decent standard of living. They had a large house and traveled to Europe every summer. Imad, on the other hand, came from a modest Christian family. His father was a simple worker, and they lived in a humble house right next to our school. Their different religious and social backgrounds, however, did not affect their friendship. Raad and Imad remained best friends even after they graduated, got married, and had children. I was really saddened when I heard their friendship had suddenly broken up.

No one knew exactly what had happened. They didn't say a thing about it, and we all respected their privacy. A few years later, I was buying something from Raad's electronic-gadget shop. He asked me whether I needed technical assistance, and I told him I had already asked for Imad's help. His face became sad when I mentioned the name. He lowered his eyes, and said, "We used to be good friends, you know." Of course I knew. Everyone did. "I couldn't put our friendship before my religion, nonetheless." I was surprised. Until then, I had not the slightest idea that religion caused their falling-out.

The feud, it turned out, started after Raad had heard

the imam at the mosque say that Muslims, unless under compelling circumstances, should not befriend nonbelievers and should avoid dealing with them in every possible way. The imam then recited a verse from the Koran to prove his point. Raad had read that verse many times before, but it was his first time contemplating its meaning and the way it could impinge on his life. Before making any drastic decisions, he needed to talk to his best friend about it.

"I asked him whether he believed in the Oneness of God, the Koran, and the message of Prophet Mohammed. I wanted to make sure that he was a believer too. At first he refused to answer and demanded to know what had made me ask those strange questions. But when I insisted to know, he said he respected all faiths including Islam, but as a baptized Christian, he wasn't allowed to conceive of Mohammed as a prophet nor the Koran as a heavenly scripture."

Raad went back to the imam for advice, and it only took the bearded man a few seconds before he ruled that the long friendship should be terminated at once. With deep regret and bitterness, Raad obeyed, and the lifetime friends never spoke to each other again. I was familiar with the verse that caused Raad and Imad's split. Actually, it may be the most-quoted verse behind Muslim bigotry worldwide. Whenever I told my online friends that being a Muslim was mistakenly associated with being resentful of the other religions, they'd immediately refute my claim with verse fifty-one from the fifth chapter in the Koran, translated to English, copied and pasted on my window. I didn't know what to say.

Only recently did I manage to have the picture cleared up a little bit. According to my Tafseer (Koran interpretation) book, in the context of early seventh-century Arabia, every tribe had to pledge allegiance to some sovereign. Some tribes solicited protection from the Romans; others, the Persians. In return, the tribesmen had to pay their protectors taxes and send warriors to fight in their wars. In Medina, where Mohammed had settled and established the nucleus of a new social and political system, the Muslims were torn between loyalty to their new leader/Prophet and their old alliances. The controversial verse was delivered at that critical transformative stage in history to stress that a Muslim's loyalty should only be to the new regime.

The Prophet had already acknowledged both Judaism and Christianity on several occasions, but he had also established a body of laws to be obeyed by his followers, which was different from that of the People of the Book. So when the Muslims of Medina came to Mohammed seeking guidance, his answer was as clear as can be: *From this day on, no Muslim should submit to laws other than the Law of Islam.* However, many people don't know that the language of the Koran—although it is Arabic—is quite different from our everyday language. The Koran I have, for instance, gives the meanings of some words in simplified Arabic on the right margin of every page. And yet I often need to dig deeper to clarify some points of confusion. At some point in time, the commandment not to take the Jews or the Christians as protectors/ leaders was confused with not taking them as friends. The misinterpretation of a single phrase resulted in a big misconception, and it still affects the lives of many people around the world. There are Muslims I know who would never touch food served by Christians even if it was certified *halal*. Their sheikhs taught them that no sharing whatsoever was acceptable.

Scene Three

Does God really love Muslims more than he loves Jews and Christians? If so, why does He mention the Jews so many times in the Koran? If we talk about somebody all the time, it only means one thing: that we care about him or her greatly, right? But God talks about the Jews with such bitterness, as though He were a broken-hearted lover. When I was child, this used to make me jealous. I repeatedly read their story in the Koran: how God had honored them—of all the peoples of the world—as His treasured chosen people, how He had sent them many messengers, and how the Jews kept disappointing Him over and over again. He abandoned them and forgave them, punished them and rewarded them.

Reading the Koranic verses about the Christians has been no less confusing. Some parts of the Koran suggest that it's okay to trust them and marry them, while other parts say they are infidels who have wandered off God's Straight Path. In one verse, Jesus beseeches God to forgive his deluded followers who thought he was God incarnate. I needed to know how, as a Muslim, I was supposed to deal with Christians, Jews, Buddhists, agnostics, and atheists. Should I accept everyone? Should I try to convert them to

Islam and fight them if they refuse? Does God really want me to do that? These questions plagued me throughout my adolescent years.

Why should I care who God loves more? Is this even my business? What is my business anyway? My thoughts and feelings about my faith were becoming scary, and I hated myself for having them. Nothing was certain anymore. *Why do I need to pray or fast? Can't God just look into my heart and tell if I'm a good person or not? Why does He allow disasters to occur, and why let the poor starve to death?* I prayed more and read the Koran more frequently, but little did that help. Deep in my heart, I sensed His presence, but I couldn't identify who He was exactly.

God names Himself in the Koran as the Beneficent, the Most Merciful, and the Light of the Heavens and the Earth. I liked that. I had no problem accepting the Islamic story of creation. I didn't mind most of the rituals either, but I did have problems understanding the many technical instructions in the Koran. I also didn't like the violent attitude—the severe corporal punishments and the discrimination against women. And why had Mohammed married so many wives? I thought maybe it was time I started exploring the other religions to find out for myself what they were really about and whether they were better, worse, or (maybe) just like Islam.

Scene Four

My first time reading the Bible was extremely confusing. I was familiar with some quotes from the New Testament:

Let he who is without sin cast the first stone. Judge not, lest ye be judged. But that was it! I asked a Christian friend to lend me her Bible. I was particularly curious to read the prophecies about Prophet Mohammed as given by Jesus Christ. In the Koran, God says both the Jews and the Christians would immediately recognize the message of Mohammed, for he is mentioned in their books. As I read, I noticed the obvious resemblance between the Bible and the Koran. But I was shocked by the fundamental differences between them as well.

The Bible is made up of two separate collections of books. The Old Testament, being the first and older collection, tells the story of Creation and the history of the Jews before the birth of Jesus, while the New Testament is more or less a biography of Christ, as narrated by his disciples, and an account of the first century of Christianity. The Koran is quite different: it's a single collection of chapters divided according to the city where they were revealed. Some chapters are therefore Meccans, while others are Medinans. Also, God in the Koran speaks in the first person. It is Him telling, commanding, forbidding, or warning. The Prophet, in this case, is a mere addressee, a mortal recipient of God's message. He should be respected and obeyed, but he's by no means a deity.

Professing a solid belief in the Oneness of God is the first and most important prerequisite for being a Muslim. God does not beget, nor was He begotten, and there is none equal to Him. Everything else in the Islamic faith may be disputed, but this statement remains non-negotiable, and is agreed upon by all the different Muslim denominations. For years I had taken it for granted that the People of the Book shared our same conception of God. But when I started reading the Gospel, I found out the Christians actually believe God is three divine persons in one nature: the Father, the Son, and the Holy Spirit.

This realization came like a punch in the face: not only were we different, we were at extreme odds! *How could they say that about God? How could they claim that the Prophet Jesus, the Son of Mary, is God's son? How dare they say God is three persons? This is sheer heresy!* I had been told that our differences were not fundamental, but now I was discovering a totally different reality. Instead of encouraging us to learn and accept other people's differences, our books and teachers pretended that differences did not exist.

Scene Five

When the school bell rang, announcing the end of a short break and the start of Islamic Education class, our merry faces turned lifeless, as if touched by a magic wand of misery. One after the other, we trudged back to our wooden desks. Our teacher walked in, read the names of our Christian schoolmates, and gave them permission to leave the room to play in the schoolyard. We jealously watched them run into the sun and fresh air while we had to spend a long time reciting and memorizing words that we would never use in our daily life. Another strange thing about those lessons is that we didn't have a particular teacher. Most of the time it would be our Arabic teacher, but whenever she was busy or absent, any other teacher would suffice. Arabic, English, or even Physical Education teachers, it didn't matter. They would just grab a textbook from one of the boys or girls in the front row and tell us to repeat after them.

I took my first lesson when I was only six. We could neither read nor write, and I remember how our teacher struggled to teach us the Five Pillars of Islam while we cried hysterically. In our next lesson, the teacher said, "We Muslims and the Jews and the Christians all worship the same God, Allah." Several years later, I was told that the people God mentioned in the last verse of the Opening chapter as *those who'd deserved His wrath* were the Jews, whereas in the same verse, *the ones who'd gone astray* were the Christians. *But why? What did they do?* I had my good Christian friends: we played, studied, and ate together. I loved their families and they loved mine. They didn't seem to be evil at all.

In fact, when I was a youngster, I sometimes thought Christianity was more interesting than Islam. It was more artistic and musical, and I loved the paintings and songs. It also seemed much less violent and easier to prac-tice compared to Islam—at the time, I didn't know the Christians hadn't always been this peaceful, nor had their rituals been this easy. The intense drama of Jesus' story was another a big attraction for me: the way he was conceived by the Holy Spirit and born of a virgin, the many miracles he performed during his time on Earth, his horrible cruci-fixion, and later, his resurrection. However, the final chapter of this fascinating drama is yet another point of disagree-ment between us and them.

Scene Six

The Islamic account of Jesus' story ends with an interesting twist: Jesus was not crucified because he was too precious to God to be left to suffer on the cross. It was made to appear to everyone as if he had been killed. But in fact, God raised Jesus up to Him. When I shared that piece of information with my Christian friends in school, I expected them to be ecstatic. I was breaking great news to them: their most beloved Jesus had not been crucified. Hooray! To my big disappointment, their faces showed hardly any enthusiasm. Baffled by their silence, I read the Koran again. God does deny the crucifixion, but He speaks vaguely about what happened on that dire day. How was it made to appear that Jesus was being crucified when he really was not, and when and how did God raise him up? We don't know.

This ambiguous realization paved the way for different readings and interpretations, the most common of which suggests that God made Judas look exactly like Jesus, and so the Roman soldiers took him to be killed on the cross instead. The hero was saved; the villain, brutally punished; it sounded perfect to me. Another theory claims the whole crucifixion was nothing but an illusion. But was it mental? Optical? Again, we have no clue. Either way, I don't think it is possible for any Christian to accept these theses simply because they negate the beliefs that have been central to most Christian churches for millennia.

First and foremost, Christianity's significant religious symbol, the cross, would be of very little value if Jesus' crucifixion proved to be a delusion. Second, and most importantly, if one agrees that Jesus was not crucified, then he also couldn't have risen from the dead on the third day, as the Gospel says. Which in turn demolishes an essential pillar of the Christian faith, the resurrection. But that's not all: this approach would not only raise a great deal of suspicion over the authenticity of the entire book, but it would also call the credibility of all the Christian apostles, disciples, and saints into question. If this happened, little would remain of the Christianity we know today. When I was younger, I asked myself, *Is this what we Muslims are supposed to be doing? Should we point out the fallacies in Christianity and Judaism so that the whole world knows Islam is the only genuine religion?*

The Koran also says the Jews and the Christians both rewrote their holy books to suit their desires and interests. I wondered if that was why I couldn't find anything about the Prophet Mohammed when I read the Bible. It all seemed incomprehensible at the time. We believe in Jesus Christ, the word and spirit of God. Unlike the Jews, we admit that he was the promised Messiah and that he was born of a virgin, whom we highly respect too. And yet, it is not the other way around: Christians do not admit that the Prophet was the messenger of God.

Back then, I didn't know rivalry had always existed between religions, especially the monotheistic ones. It sometimes hides behind veil of mutual respect and acceptance, but the older religions have always denied the new ones. The Jews refused to recognize Christianity, the Christians then refused to recognize Islam, and even the Muslims now refuse to recognize Baha'ism because the Koran says

Mohammed is the Seal of the Prophets, which means no other messenger will be sent to mankind until the end of time. The Prophet himself predicted that many liars would claim prophet-hood after his death and warned Muslims against believing them. The newer religions, on the other hand, insist that they have been sent by God to rectify the older ones. After terrible conflict and bloodshed, they've settled on a begrudging admission of coexistence, but never a complete recognition.

Scene Seven

"What Christ says, and what your Mohammed says, are like two rays from the same lamp. The difference between you and us is no bigger than this line," said the dark-skinned man with the frizzy grey beard. He was playing the role of the old king of Abyssinia on the screen, and in this scene he drew a line on the floor with the base of his scepter. I still remember the solemn sound the staff made as it scratched across that stone floor. It was summertime in London, my parents had heard about the film from their friends, and they took my brothers and me to watch it in a theater not far from Piccadilly Circus. After we settled in our seats and before the lights faded out, I noticed a European couple in front of me deep-kissing. Even at my young age then, I couldn't help wondering, *Has someone told them this was a romantic film?!*

I had already watched several Egyptian films in Baghdad about the story of Islam, but they were all very poorly executed. The acting was pretentious, the make-up and the costumes very bad, the scripts cheesy, and likewise the soundtracks. All the same, they were shown on television on every religious holiday. Many people could have recited the lines of dialogue by heart. *The Message*, however, was different from all the other historical films I had watched. It was the first high-budget production about the life of the Prophet to be made in two versions with two different casts. One was in Arabic and the other in English for audiences in the West and non-Arab Muslim countries. The leaking news of the film had stirred a heated controversy even before it premiered in London. It was banned in Egypt and Saudi Arabia because although the filmmakers had been keen on keeping up with the Islamic code of not showing the image of the Prophet, it was the first time in the history of Arabic films that characters so close to Mohammed were personified on screen. Hamza, Mohammed's uncle, was the pivotal character in the film, brilliantly portrayed in the English version by two-time Oscar winner Anthony Quinn.

All I can say about that experience is that it left me awestruck. Mouth agape, I remember being frozen in my seat through much of the film's three hours. The music, written by French composer Maurice Jarre, was nominated for an Academy Award for best original score in 1978, and even though more than thirty years have passed since its first release, it can still be heard on several religious radio and television programs throughout the Islamic world. To this day, it touches me profoundly every time I listen to it. I have to admit that I owe much of my early knowledge of Islam to that film. Neither my parents' talks nor my

Islamic Education classes at school could have given me the amount of information *The Message* was able to deliver in only a few hours.

I found an interesting article by Mark Steyn in *The Atlantic*, claiming—according to Queen Noor of Jordan—the Pentagon bought a hundred thousand copies of *The Message* to show to U.S. troops before they left for Afghanistan. Strangely enough, the Syrian-American director of the film, Moustapha Akkad (who dedicated a great deal of his life and career to explaining the peaceful nature of Islam to the world), was killed with his daughter in November 2005 in a terrorist bombing by Al Qaeda in Jordan.

When we suffered persecution in Mecca, Mohammed told us go to Abyssinia, the land of a righteous king, where no man is wronged. These words of the Prophet's envoy to the king, among many others from *The Message* shaped my childhood perception of the relationship between Islam and Christianity. Another scene from the film showed a Christian man from Nineveh consoling the Prophet and offering him grapes after the people of Taif had thrown stones at him and chased him out of their town. My romantic perception was severely shaken when I heard the Koranic verses that hinted the Christians' infidelity and hypocrisy. It gave me the shudders to imagine my Christian friends being burned in the eternal flames of hell, screaming out for help while the fire consumed their bodies. *Will God listen to my plea if I begged Him to forgive them?* From the bottom of my heart, I hoped that He would.

The Prophet was born centuries after the fourth canonical Gospel had been written. Christianity had mostly settled down into the body of faith we know now when Mohammed received his first revelation from Gabriel. So if the Christians were infidels, then why did the Prophet trust them that much in the beginning? Why did he, of all the lands around Arabia, instruct the early Muslims to seek refuge in Abyssinia—a Christian land ruled by a Christian monarch who believed in the divine nature of Jesus and in the Holy Trinity of God? This was another point that needed clarification.

Scene Eight

"So where are you from?" the taxi driver asked me only seconds after I stepped into his car. We had barely exchanged traditional greetings—*Alsalamu alaikum* (Peace be upon you)—and I had just told him my destination, which was more than enough for him to guess I wasn't a local. "Don't you agree that life in Iraq under Saddam was much better than it is now?"

I could see that question coming from the moment I told him I came from Iraq. By that time, I knew there were other questions waiting in line, and I had a good supply of ready-to-give answers.

"Yes, it's very bad now, but it was very bad under Saddam too," I said.

Over the past seven decades, millions of Palestinians have fled to the east bank of the River Jordan. It's hard to get accurate numbers because many of them have been granted Jordanian citizenship, and hundreds of thousands more still live there as refugees. It is believed that more than half of Jordan's inhabitants today are of Palestinian origins. I have many good Palestinian friends in Jordan and we get along very well, but I know too well that when it comes to Saddam Hussein, it's no use trying to convince them that he was no hero.

In the years that followed the Iraqi invasion of Kuwait in 1990 until his downfall in 2003, Saddam provided Jordan with free oil in return for political support when Iraq was entirely cut off from the world. Palestinian students in Iraq were admitted to the university of their choice, regardless of their school grades, and their families enjoyed generous financial assistance and privileges at a time when the Iraqis were struggling to survive. Children were dying of diseases and malnutrition, and many families were selling off their precious heirlooms cheaply just to make ends meet.

Saddam talked about the liberation of Al-Quds (Jerusalem) in almost all of his rhetorical speeches. The Iraqi media constantly compared him to the historical leader Salah Al-Din Al-Ayoubi, born in the twelfth century in the Iraqi province of Tikrit—where Saddam was born too. Salah Al-Din is best known for defeating the Crusaders and retaking Jerusalem in 1187. While neither I nor any Iraqi I know would buy such propaganda, many Palestinians, Arabs, and other Muslims did. They truly believed Saddam was going to liberate the Holy Land from Israeli occupation—especially after he fired several Scud missiles at Israeli cities during the First Gulf War. He also paid tens of thousands of U.S. dollars to the families of Palestinian suicide bombers, and "Palestine belongs to the Arabs" were his last words before he was executed. In brief, they had every reason to love Saddam and revere him first as a glorious hero and later as a legendary martyr. They even name their children after him. I smiled ironically when I caught a glimpse of a small picture stuck on the car's dashboard: Saddam, of course.

"Not another Starbucks!" The Palestinian driver exclaimed as we passed by a new branch of the popular coffee chain just opening. Why would a café bother a taxi driver? I knew that Starbucks—along with other Western coffeehouse brands—had gained popularity among Westernized Arab youth after the huge success of the American television sitcom *Friends*. Just like Ross, Rachel, Monica, Chandler, Phoebe, and Joey used to do in the original series, young Arabs were now chatting, reading, and flirting while they sipped coffee on the comfortable couches of their neighborhood Starbucks. Amman alone has several branches. "Did you read what they are saying about it on the Internet?"

I was baffled for a few seconds, but then I remembered an email I had received a long time ago. Many Muslims believed that Starbucks, as well as McDonald's, were donating a large portion of their massive revenues worldwide to support the Jewish state of Israel's offensive against the Palestinians. Yes, I was aware of those rumors, but I had also read that Starbucks had released a statement saying that they were unequivocally false.

"And you *believed* them?"

Clearly annoyed by my ignorance, the cabby went on: "Look at their logo! Can't you see it's an image of an ancient Jewish goddess?"

Now this is getting really ridiculous, I thought. I tried to explain to him that even if we were to assume that Starbucks was indeed funding Israel, their logo couldn't have possibly been inspired by a Jewish goddess because there was no such thing as a Jewish goddess!

"The Jews are monotheistic. Just like us Muslims, they worship the One God, and they don't even believe in the Christian Trinity, so they definitely can't have a goddess." Still, he was unconvinced. "You know what? If they are really this smart and powerful, then good for them!" I regretted my words immediately after saying them. He may have had family and friends living hellish lives every day inside Israel, or lost a brother or a sister in the ever-raging conflicts between the Palestinians and the Israelis there. I should have known better.

"What?" he exclaimed again, in an unbelieving tone this time. "Good for the Jews?" He repeated my words to make sure that he hadn't misheard them. No sane Arab-Muslim would ever say what I'd just said.

I had to make a quick explanation: "For the past sixty years, both the Israelis and the Palestinians have been receiving enormous donations from countries, organizations, and individuals around the world. Look at how the Israelis have invested their money and how developed Israel is today. Look at the high standard of living most Israelis enjoy, and let's compare that to the poverty and inhuman conditions many, if not most, Palestinians are living under. Could you please tell me where have the billions of dollars gone?

"Unfortunately, corrupt Palestinian politicians have been diverting good amounts of those donations into their personal foreign bank accounts, and they've spent whatever was left to fund the inter-Palestinian clashes that only caused the people further misery and widened the rift between them. We can't blame the Jews for that too, can we?"

It may sound naïve, but I honestly believe that the Arabs have much to learn from their enemies. The survivors of a horrific genocide in World War II Europe managed to rise from the ashes of their ordeal to build a modern democratic state amidst the dictatorships in the Middle East. Whether we like it or not, Jewish assets and brains control much of the world media, banking, industry, and scientific research nowadays. Emotions aside, I find the Jews' perseverance and solidarity worthy of admiration. I hope I made my point clear to the Palestinian taxi driver before I got out of the car to meet some friends at the mall. Not very far from the main entrance, I saw another crowded Starbucks.

Scene Nine

My parents were excited when I told them I could search out their old friends and relatives on the Internet. I watched their faces beam when they saw pictures of people they thought they'd never see again, and I couldn't help smiling when they muttered, "Look how old they've become!" I even managed to get them some phone numbers and had a tear in my eye when they started talking and sobbing on the phone after many long years. However, their fascination dwindled after we had searched all the names they could think of. And sadly, we found out that several of their old friends had long since passed away.

"Okay, who else do you want me to look up?"

My mother seemed a bit reluctant. She shook her head and said, "No, I don't think you'd ever be able to find Evelyn. She was my best friend when I was a child." I didn't know my mother had had a friend named Evelyn. I'd never heard her mention the name before. But she was right, I couldn't have possibly found Evelyn just by typing in my search box: *Evelyn-Iraqi-Jew-left-Iraq-with-family-more-than-sixty-years-ago*. That was all the information I could get from my mother about Evelyn.

"No, I don't think we stand a chance," I told my mother, who couldn't remember Evelyn's surname because they had been only little girls when they became friends.

The last memory my mother has of her Jewish friend is soaked with tears. Evelyn stood trembling next to her mother, both of them crying. They came to say goodbye to my mother and grandmother after they had been advised to leave Iraq over the 1948 war and its repercussions on the entire region. My grandmother offered to host them in her house, but they both knew it wasn't going to work. The two little girls—my mother and Evelyn—hugged and wept as if they'd known it was the last time they were ever going to see each other. In retaliation for the deprivation of the

Palestinian people of their land and the declaration of the
state of Israel on what was until then known as Palestine,
the Iraqi Jews, as well as other Arab Jews, were forced to
leave the countries where they and their ancestors had lived
for many generations. Their possessions were looted. On an
emotional rampage, the masses decided that all Jews should
suffer the injustice Israel had inflicted on the Palestinians.

Except for a few Jewish families scattered here and
there, Iraq was a Jew-free country when I was born in 1969.
We were taught in school that Jews are spiteful, treach-
erous, and miserly by nature. They mercilessly killed our
Palestinian brothers, uprooted their olive trees, demolished
their houses, and drove them out of their homeland. Every
single morning we chanted anthems of liberation and return.
I remember myself at one of our school celebrations taking
the stage dressed up like a soldier and pointing a plastic gun
at the Israeli enemy. I was so proud to do that. Our childish
drawings illustrated hands signing victory with a Palestinian
ensign and the Dome of the Rock Mosque poorly depicted
in the background. In our English Literature classes in high
school, out of all of Shakespeare's work, we were taught *The
Merchant of Venice*. Questions that revolved around the
evil character of Shylock the Jew had become the standard
in every year's final exams. But our hatred for the Jews and
everything Jewish wasn't confined to our school walls.

Many films talked about the heroism of Arab soldiers
in the battlefields. The leading actors were always ready to
die for the noblest cause—that is, freeing Palestine from
the filthy Zionists. Our radio stations incessantly broadcast

songs and poems of nostalgia for the beloved cities of Jerusalem, Jaffa, and Galilee, whereas the news on television showed disturbing scenes of Palestinian women wailing over the loss of their sons, brothers, or husbands, shot by Israeli soldiers. We couldn't but hate the Jewish aggressors. And we did, wholeheartedly.

When I grew up, I tried to find impartial resources for Judaism, but there were hardly any left in the Baghdadi bookstores I searched. Endless editions of *The Protocols of the Elders of Zion* filled the shelves. I had read the book already, but I was looking for something less judgmental and more informative. I wanted to understand why the Jews were so evil and whether their mischief was innate or acquired. I looked for the Torah, but I couldn't find it either, so I finally resolved to reading the Old Testament as the closest alternative to the Jewish scriptures. It was then that I realized the Jews, as well as the Christians, believe that Isaac, not Ishmael—as mentioned in the Koran—was the son Abraham had been commanded to sacrifice.

Scene Ten

After performing my morning prayer one day, I opened the Koran randomly and came across this verse. Moses was addressing the people of Israel: *O my people! Enter the holy land which God has destined for you, and retreat not or defeated you shall be* (5.21). The Israelites disobeyed Moses, and for that, God punished them with forty years in the wilderness. I don't know why it didn't happen earlier, but it was my first time deeply reflecting on the meaning of that verse. I read it again, and went to see what my Tafseer book had to say about the incident. I was still holding onto the slight chance that Moses could have been talking about some other holy land in his speech. But no, the Tafseer book assured me that he had in fact meant Palestine. I was baffled because that verse clearly supported the Jewish claim to the Palestinian land. And by clearly, I mean, it was different from the first promise God made to Abraham, that he and his descendants would inherit the land, which in turn was a big controversy.

It is difficult to determine who are the promised descendants of Abraham, given the vague reference and the billions of people who could claim the title. First, we need to figure out if *descendants* refers to Abraham's spiritual followers or his biological offspring. While the former may include all human beings who worship the One God, the latter is confined to the children of Abraham's two sons Isaac (the father of the Jews) and Ishmael (the father of the Arabs). However, Jewish and Christian scholars would argue that the promise was given to Isaac's children alone, not Ishmael's. I personally don't think this makes much sense, yet even if we are to accept the assumption, we still have to sort out other problems like conversion. Many Jews have converted to Christianity and Islam over the centuries, which means their brood could be among the hundreds of thousands of Palestinian refugees denied the right to live on their own ancestral land. Does apostasy revoke the promise to the land? I have no clue.

Another common misconception among pro-Israel

Westerners is categorizing the Arabic animus against the Israelis as anti-Semitism. This may have been true with the Nazis, but it cannot be the case with the Arabs: we are as Semitic as the Jews themselves. Both peoples are descended from Noah's son Shem, so Prophet Mohammed was as Semitic as Moses or Jesus. In brief, I don't think religion can provide a solution to the conflict in the Middle East, precisely because it was religion that created the problem between children of Abraham in the first place. Religion and politics have kept the flames of hatred burning for ages.

Scene Eleven

In 1917, the United Kingdom's government decided to enable the Jewish people to establish a national home in Palestine. We don't really know whether there was a religious reason for issuing the Balfour Declaration—named after then Foreign Secretary Arthur Balfour. The document states, "nothing shall be done which may prejudice the civil and religious rights of existing non-Jewish communities in Palestine." Our history teacher at school told us that British imperialism aimed at implanting an alien body into the heart of the Arab world to abort people's dreams of unity. "Our unity would have threatened their strategic interests in our region," he said.

I remembered that teacher years later when I read in the newspaper that while visiting Jordan in 1984, Queen Elizabeth acknowledged the tragedy that has befallen the Palestinian people and promised that her government would "continue to support all constructive efforts to

achieve a peaceful, just, and lasting solution to this problem."
Nevertheless, the Queen did not say anything about her
country's role in creating the Palestinian tragedy. I guess
the true intention behind Britain's infamous declaration to
the Jews in 1917 will remain a mystery, but little does that
matter now. What really matters today is that Israel exists
and has been here for more than sixty years.

Shortly after the Balfour Declaration, Jewish immi-
grants, mainly from Europe, started arriving in Palestine.
The Arabs' response to the challenge was quite emotional.
Instead of defending the Palestinians' lawful right to live and
maintain sovereignty over their land, religion was involved.
The strong legal case was transformed into a controversial
religious feud between the Muslims and the Jews. Let's face
it: Islam is the most recent of the three monotheistic faiths.
And while many Jewish and Christian messengers and
disciples had lived, died, and were buried in that land, the
Muslims had only arrived there five years after the Prophet's
death. Al-Aqsa mosque was built many years after that
on the site believed to be where Mohammed ascended to
heaven in his Night Journey.

Although the majority is Muslim, Christians have always
made up a considerable number of the total Palestinian population. Hundreds of thousands of Palestinian Christians,
both inside and outside of their country, suffered and are still
suffering the same hardships as Palestinian Muslims. Their
lands have been equally confiscated, their mobility equally
restricted. But unlike Islam, Christianity was born there, and
one generation after another of Christian Palestinians lived

on the land from the time of Jesus until this day. Not many people know that Hanan Ashrawi—the former spokeswoman for the Palestinian delegation to the Middle East peace talks, and the renowned member of the Palestinian Liberation Organization (PLO)—is a Christian; likewise George Habash—the founder of the Popular Front for the Liberation of Palestine (PFLP), which pioneered the hijacking of airplanes to promote political causes during the late sixties. I have many Christian friends myself, but not a single one of them is supportive of Israel.

The creation of the state of Israel in Palestine, in my opinion, was one of the worst injustices of the twentieth century. Again, little does that matter now. Most of the Israeli youth today were born in Israel, and many of their parents and grandparents too. We cannot collectively punish them for what the early Jewish settlers did to the Palestinians almost a hundred years ago—although Israel has often used collective punishments against the Palestinians. But it just doesn't make sense. We can't expect the Israelis to pack and leave their towns and cities. Where would they go? It's only natural for them to fight and try to defend themselves when they are attacked, but wars and violence have already proved to be futile.

Three wars have failed to liberate Palestine. Israel came out of each war with more and more occupied lands in Egypt, Syria, and Jordan. It was soon clear to everyone that the West was not going to allow the Arabs victory over the Hebrew state, and yet the wars didn't stop. As a matter of fact, the only land we have ever managed to retrieve is that which was redeemed through talks with the Israelis, so maybe this could give us a hint. I wish the Palestinians and the Israelis would sit down and negotiate based on their present and the future of their children rather than on the suffering of their fathers. Religious debates aside, there are humanitarian priorities to discuss. People need food, houses, jobs, medication, and decent infrastructure. As a Muslim Arab, it is difficult for me to say that, and I only can imagine how difficult it will be for the Palestinian people to give up their lawful right of return to their beloved lands. It's unquestionably bitter, but I think it's a cost worth paying for peace and for providing a better future for their children.

Scene Twelve

I would be lying if I said I knew exactly what Danish cartoonist Kurt Westergaard was thinking when he drew his infamous cartoons about the Prophet for the *Jyllands-Posten* newspaper in 2005. But I can't say that I'm clueless, either. After I read about them in a newspaper in Baghdad, I was curious to take a peek at the drawings. It's really hard to describe the way I felt when I saw them online. Like millions of Muslims around the world, I was offended. I couldn't help but take it personally, although it wasn't meant to be taken that way. (Well, maybe it was.)

The most talked-about cartoon from the twelve-piece collection by Westergaard and other Danish cartoonists depicted Mohammed as a stern-faced man—who looked like an Indian Maharaja to me!—with a time bomb in his turban. Another one showed him with an unsheathed sword in his hand and two women shrouded in black standing behind him. The women's eyes were wide open, but the man's eyes—the Prophet's, supposedly—were censored with a black bar exactly the size and shape of the eye-slots in the women's veils. The symbolism was quite subtle, but these cartoons angered a quarter of the world's population. An enormous campaign to boycott all Danish products commenced, and violent protests broke out throughout the Islamic world. But it wasn't the first time the West had provoked the feelings of the Muslim masses.

Almost a year earlier, Theo van Gogh, a Dutch film director, was brutally murdered in Amsterdam by a fanatic Muslim shortly after the broadcast of van Gogh's film *Submission* on national television. The ten-minute film was written by the controversial Somali-born Dutch parliament member Ayaan Hirsi Ali about violations of Muslim women's rights, something Ayaan had experienced firsthand. *Submission* showed Koranic verses written on the bodies of praying women who wore nothing but transparent black veils. It was more than enough to enrage the Dutch Muslims and cost the film's director his life. Many Muslims, including my own family, couldn't understand why the Westerners seemed so fond of blaspheming our faith and hurting our religious feelings.

The misunderstanding, however, appears to be mutual. European artists, on the one hand, believe that no person or value is above criticism. They bask in a long tradition of satire that spares nothing and no one. They criticize God, religion, monarchs, clerics, and politicians. They don't understand why Muslims are so sensitive to this form of humor. We Muslims, on the other hand, have a very special bond with the Prophet. We don't worship him the way Christians worship Jesus, and we know very well that he was a mortal messenger, but he is like a patriarch in every Muslim home. We respect him, obey him, and try to emulate him at all times. So naturally it *does* offend us when someone ridicules Mohammed or makes fun of him.

I admire the Prophet but I can't claim that I fully understand his character. There are things about him that I revere, but there are other things I just cannot fathom. And while I can freely share my admiration for him with everyone—and would likely get some very good credit for it by doing so—I can't similarly share my questions and confusion. I often ask myself whether this is cowardice, hypocrisy, or just respect, but I still don't have an answer.

It eventually dawned on me the offensive cartoons had used the Prophet's image to reflect our own. The Danish cartoonists looked around and saw Muslims talking about peace and compassion while their deeds screamed otherwise. They saw Muslim men on television say *Allahu akbar* (God is great) before chopping off the heads of bound, kneeling captives. They saw Muslim men treat Muslim women disrespectfully, beating them and forcing them into obedience in the name of Allah and the Prophet, and when they refused to comply, killing them. The irony was everywhere, an obvious target for the cartoonists.

I was talking with a friend from New Zealand about the role the media played in emphasizing the stereotypical image of Muslims as terrorists. He said, "You can't expect news anchors to tell people, 'It's been a quiet day in Kabul: nothing bad happened,' or 'We'd like to introduce a Muslim man from Iraq who has neither kidnapped nor killed anyone!'" I guess he is right. It is the media's job to fish for controversies and atrocities. The media can't turn a blind eye to them whenever and wherever they happen. Sadly, they so often do. I remember when I started corresponding with literary agents about publishing a book I had written on my life in Iraq during Saddam's reign, one of them asked me, "Does your book have screaming stories of killing, rape, and torture?" And when I answered no, I never heard back from him.

Whether we like it or not, this fast-food culture influences every aspect of our lives. From books to films, music, and even appearances, everything should be extra-crunchy and crispy on the outside, creamy on the inside. Come to think of it, who would want to miss the thrill of watching collapsing towers and slain victims to listen to the boring words of moderate Muslims? In the darkness of the movie theater and with the breathtaking suspense on the screen, people love to munch buttery caramel popcorn. They don't crave green salad.

Beyond the Threshold

When someone told me there are people in India who worship cows, I chuckled. I thought it was a funny joke. But when I realized it was not a joke, I stopped laughing, and a sense of bewilderment took over: *But that's nonsense.*

Don't they know cows are only animals? How could they worship animals? At that time, I was just learning that not all people were Muslims, Christians, or Jews. I could understand worshipping God/Allah, but cows? I wanted to get to know those people, listen to them, and learn more about their beliefs. After the war, when I had the privilege of an uncensored Internet, the dream finally became a reality. I must say it was an eye-opener.

I realized how deficient my previous conception about those people and their beliefs was. An online Hindu friend told me they don't worship cows in the same way we Muslims or other monotheists worship God. Instead, they have a rather special affection for cows because they represent the giving nature of life. They give us so much and demand very little from us in return. To be honest, I'd never thought about cows this way before, and I'm not sure if that explanation has anything to do with my sudden loss of craving for meat in general. It was quite interesting to understand the meaning of the strong bond Hindus share with their animals and trees.

In a similar way, the books I read on Buddhism, Taoism, Kabbalah, and Sufism have all illuminated dark corners of my consciousness and reshaped my perception of life and religion altogether. Today, I like to think of the Divine as a beautiful garden surrounded by a fence with several entrance gates. All the gates are open, but—sadly—not all people dare to go inside because bigotry nails them down and makes them dwell in the thresholds. But the threshold is one thing, and the garden is another. I made up my mind to go inside because I don't want to remain at the entrance. I knew the first step wasn't going to be easy, but it was definitely worthwhile.

Chapter 11

What's under the Garment of Piety?

O CHILDREN OF ADAM! WE HAVE BESTOWED CLOTHING UPON YOU TO COVER YOUR NAKEDNESS, AS WELL AS TO BE AN ADORN-MENT. BUT THE GARMENT OF PIETY IS THE BEST. THAT IS A REVELATION OF GOD TO REMEMBER.

(7.26)

Whenever I'm at a train station or a bus stop, or just stuck in traffic, I often try to amuse myself by watching people. I look at their faces and think of the stories their smiles or grimaces might be hiding or exposing. I am sure I'm not the only one who does this. People watch people all the time because it's easier to look outside than to look inside. Among the faces I find myself scrutinizing the most are those of covered girls and women.

It's not an easy choice for contemporary Muslim women to withdraw from mainstream carnal culture and accept being less attractive to men in an age where being sexy is probably the highest-regarded quality by so many people. Men and women are struggling to achieve the perfect body, hair, face, and dress. We want to have them all but our bodies have their limits, which we keep pushing over the edge. Hence, the depression, the eating disorders, and the growing obsession with plastic surgery.

That being said, I'm not sure covering is always an expression of deep spirituality or a withdrawal from mainstream carnal culture. Is it courage, a means of escaping the competition, or just a social trend? I'm not sure I know *what* it is.

Scene One

One afternoon in Amman, I had to go to the bank. Inside, a number of beautiful girls were seated behind the front counter. Flawless, hair done to perfection, there was not a single straying strand on any of their heads. Their makeup was perfect too. The front-desk girls smiled heart-warming smiles, and a lovely fragrance filled the air around them. Not too strong, not too faint. When I went upstairs to finish some paperwork, the perfect scene changed. Women who were less smiley, less in-shape, and much more serious-looking replaced the Barbie-like girls. Oh, and they were all covering their hair!

It was rush hour when I completed my transaction, so it was very difficult to find a vacant taxi. I waved and waved but to no avail. Under the glare of the afternoon sun, I couldn't tell whether oncoming taxis were occupied or not, so I kept waving nonetheless. Taxi after taxi passed me by with covered women sitting in their back seats. *It must be a coincidence*, I first thought, but it went on for quite a while, almost an hour. My intuition told me there would be another woman wearing *hijab* in the next taxi, and indeed there was. And then another, and another.

Not only in taxis, covered women were actually every-where around me, as if I had been transported to another land, the land where all women wore *hijab*! I watched them walk, shop, and sip coffee. All covered. I looked at the bank to make sure I wasn't dreaming, but it had closed. Where had all the gorgeous uncovered girls at the front desk gone? It occurred to me that if I walked inside again, I'd find them covered too. *The hot sun is messing up my head,* I thought, and smiled at my own absurdity. Had I just imagined those uncovered women? Of course I knew *hijab* was popular among Muslim girls and women, but I hadn't known it was *that* popular. Just as I recognized reality for what it was, I also found it extremely weird!

Scene Two

Three men walked into the restaurant, with three women following closely. One of the men said something to the waiter, who nodded and led them to two separate tables—one for the men, another for the women. Their tables happened to be next to mine. All three women wore black *burqa*s that covered their bodies entirely. Even their hands were covered with long black satin gloves. But while they saw people through their black veils, other people could not see their faces. I was curious to see how they were going to eat. When the food arrived, they sat facing the wall. With every single bite, they lifted only a small part of the veil to allow food to pass. This went on until they'd finished eating, but then came dessert. I couldn't stand the sight anymore. It was getting on my nerves. I paid my bill and left quickly.

But why don't I like *hijab*s and *burqa*s? I often wonder. Don't Muslim women have the right to choose the type of attire that fits with their religious beliefs? Isn't the freedom of dress a basic human right? I must admit that I feel a twinge of guilt over my dislike for women's covering. First, because I always try to stay away from judging people and interfering in their personal affairs. And second, because it's become such a solid conviction among most Muslims today that all Muslim women must cover their hair and follow a certain dress code. So much so that if one were to suggest otherwise, he or she would be instantly accused of heresy.

Am I just being nostalgic for my childhood years when women did not wear *hijab*s and life seemed much happier without it? But *hijab*s aren't necessarily dark and dull. I mean, unlike the black *burqa*s I saw at the restaurant, *hijab*s can be very colorful. Head covers today come in endless fabrics, patterns, and shapes. There are endless ways to wrap and accessorize them with beads, shiny sequins, flowers, or even feathers. Some of the covered women I have seen on the streets looked much sexier than simple-looking, uncovered girls. Others are eccentric: I remember seeing a covered woman at the Dubai airport, who had wrapped her hair with a huge piece of cloth. I thought she must have had a brain tumor! But eccentric or not, if it's a woman's wish to cover, it's fine with me. It's her life and her choice. I'm only uncomfortable when people start using their appearance to gain profits at my expense, deeming themselves worthy of all the worldly and heavenly blessings, while others, who don't look like them, are not.

Scene Three

While driving home from the military unit where we were both serving, my devout friend Adham decided to put me to a test. He lived near my place, so we carpooled together every afternoon except for the days when one of us happened to be on duty. I didn't know Adham was a fanatic until the day I heard him tell our friends at the unit to change the radio station from pop music to the Holy Koran station, or switch the radio off altogether. Before we reached his house, out of the blue—or maybe he had planned it, I don't know—Adham said, "When a girl wears *hijab* she looks as beautiful as a blossoming rose. Don't you agree?"

I couldn't help smiling. It was summertime and the heat was suffocating. Even with the car's air conditioner turned to maximum power, we were both soaked in sweat. Just trying to imagine how difficult it must be for a covered girl to walk in the street in this obscenely hot weather with a perspiring scalp wrapped in layers of cloth made me sweat even more. I knew if I told Adham what I was thinking, he'd say the summer heat was nothing compared to the heat of hellfire in the afterlife. "Well, if it makes them happy, then good for them." With someone like him, I had to choose my words very carefully. I tried my best.

"What? Did you say happy?" His tone was bursting with aggression.

"Listen, Adham, I really don't want to go through this, but if you insist, then fine." I felt exhausted, but I wasn't willing to make more compromises. "With all respect to your beliefs, I think decency is an attitude rather than a hair cover. A girl, any girl, can be seductive even when shrouded with black cloth. And she can be chaste and decent without any. It's their personal choice, after all." I only realized how far I'd gone when I looked at Adham and saw that a storm was about to blow up.

"What are you saying?" His face was beet-red. "All

Muslim women must cover their bodies and hair except for the face and hands according to the Holy Koran and the teachings of the Prophet, peace be upon him. If there is any choice, then it's a choice between being a Muslim or not."

I don't know why, but I had the feeling that he was enjoying what he was going to tell me next. His tone was lower but not in any way less aggressive. There was a ghost of a smile on his face. Carefully stressing every word, he said, "If you deny the laws of the Koran, then you have committed apostasy, and it would be lawful for any Muslim to shed your blood, unless you repent."

That was my first personal encounter with extremist Islam. So extremist that my life was threatened just because I couldn't see the point of covering for Muslim women. I dropped Adham off at his house, wondering what he would have said had I told him about my thoughts on conversion or polygamy!

Scene Four

We were lucky to have grown up in a healthy environment. And by *healthy*, I mean that my brother and I, as well as our friends, had the chance to study, play, and socialize with girls freely inside and outside of our elementary school. This changed when we moved to high school, where mixing was not allowed. But even then, we still got to meet and hang out with girls at social clubs and in our houses. It really wasn't that big a deal at the time, and we all took it for granted. As I said, our childhood was a healthy one. But it seems like ancient history now.

Many Muslim parents nowadays call for gender segre-gation in all levels of education, starting with elementary schools. This has already been done for years in several Muslim countries' schools. But where would the little boys learn to deal with girls in an entirely sexually separate society? Why alienate them from one another at such an early age? I don't understand the point of it. Supporters say it's the law of God, and God's law should be obeyed without argument. It is not my goal to argue, but I need to ask ques-tions in order to understand and develop convictions. Then I can obey. Unfortunately, some Muslims out there, including my friend Adham, would call this sacrilege. They would not hesitate to kill, or threaten to kill, those who adopt this approach.

Some parents force their girls to wear *hijab* from a very early age, as young as three or four. Now even if we assume that covering is a must for all Muslim females—few scholars disagree with that—it is only demanded of girls when they reach puberty, not little children. Parents know that already, but they say it's easier for a girl to grow up covering than to make her adapt to it when she is older and more rebellious. It may be easier, but is it fair?

Scene Five

My family wasn't totally immune to change when its winds started hitting. *Hijab* took its toll on three genera-tions of females in my household. My sister was the first. She wanted to cover her hair when she was still studying in high school—a Catholic convent high school. It was the late seventies, and only old rural women covered their heads back then. I remember that everyone was shocked when my sister broke the news to my parents.

"Religion, as I see it, is an inner obligation. If I do my work wholeheartedly, if I'm good to the people around me, then I am religious," my father told my sister quietly. His words seemed to convince her. She forgot about covering for years until the day she discovered that her only daughter was covering in secret.

My niece was ten. And just like all the girls her age, she loved to emulate her mother. She talked like her, laughed like her, and even used the same gestures. But while almost all the other girls' mothers in her class covered their hair, her mother didn't. My niece was showing us some pictures they'd taken in school when we noticed that she was covered in one of the shots. When my sister asked her about it, she kept silent. It turned out that all the girls had been covering during Ramadan and my niece thought it would have upset us if she covered like them. She didn't want to be the black sheep of her class, though. She secretly used a scarf my sister had bought her for the Koran-reading lessons, and she took it off the moment she left school.

Deep inside, my niece felt inferior to her friends because she wasn't covered like them, and in her own way, she decided to amend. It really broke my heart to hear her say that. Had it been her true desire to cover, we wouldn't have stood in her way. I wanted her to know that, so I took her out for a walk, and we talked about *hijab* as well as many other things. Shortly after that incident, my sister started wearing *hijab* like the other mothers. But only for several months. When she decided to leave Iraq after the war in 2003, one of her friends advised her to take off her headscarf during the trip to the Jordanian border. It wasn't safe for covered Iraqi women to go through the many U.S. military checkpoints. My sister took it off and has not worn it since.

Just a few months before that, my mother had come back from a pilgrimage to Mecca with my father. She had made up her mind about covering prior to leaving, and she remained covered for five years afterwards.

"They're not going to leave me alone," she told me. "People will say, *shame on this old woman who has gone to Mecca and came back bare-headed.*"

This, however, wasn't the case thirty or forty years ago. Several of my mother's friends had made the pilgrimage to Mecca, yet they never covered. Many things have changed over the past decades. And my mother, always careful about maintaining a spotless reputation, didn't mind making compromises when necessary.

Scene Six

Amman is probably one of the few remaining liberal cities in the Arab world. It might not be as liberal as Beirut, but then, Beirut has never been a typical Arabic/Islamic city. Let's say Amman is somewhere between the two extremes: Beirut and Riyadh. It's a city where one can see all types of Muslims on the streets, and non-Muslims too. This colorful scene, however, may be at risk of extinction given the growing calls for all Muslims to adopt what is being promoted throughout the Islamic world as the Muslim man's or woman's ideal appearance.

Even in liberal Amman, separation rules apply to most of the city's gyms, except for the luxury hotels and resorts frequented by foreigners. The mixing of genders is strictly prohibited in the gym's different facilities. It doesn't stop at locker rooms and showers: there are also separate workout areas and swimming pools for men and women. The only chance for them to meet is at the gym's main entrance, but never beyond.

I usually saw a group of bearded men working out in T-shirts and Bermuda shorts at the gym where I swam every morning. They started the day by exercising on treadmills. Just before hopping on the machines, they took out small Korans from their gym bags and placed them on the treadmills' monitors. They loved to read the Holy Book (which was really unnecessary) while they exercised and sweated heavily. The gym supervisor used to mute all the television screens tuned to Al Jazeera news from six to nine in the morning to play Koran-recitation CDs.

When the bearded group finished with the treadmills, the swimming pool would be their next destination. Still in their Bermuda shorts, they gathered in one circle with their beards floating on the surface of the water. They loved to tackle tough issues like death and the afterlife, the torture of the grave, and hell. Sometimes they discussed less substantial matters like whether it was preferable for old men to dye their grey beards with henna, the way the Prophet used to do—or is believed to have done. One morning, I listened to them talk while I swam, and their discussion took me back to a Friday sermon I had attended long years ago in Baghdad. The imam urged us to imitate the Prophet in every possible way: "The way he, peace be upon him, prayed, fasted, talked, walked, dressed, ate, and even cleaned himself or treated his wives, is a school of virtue for every Muslim to learn from," he said.

Indeed, what are prophets but teachers? I thought. But then, in order to prove his point, the imam told us a weird story. The Muslim army was facing strong resistance before conquering Egypt. To be more precise, *opening Egypt* was the exact term he used. The army leader took a moment to reflect. "Why are we not victorious? It must be God's way of telling us that we have strayed from the righteous path and the Prophet's teachings." All of a sudden, it dawned on him that his soldiers had stopped cleaning their teeth with *miswak*s. A *miswak* or *siwak* is a natural toothbrush made from the twigs of native trees. The ancient Arabs had been using *miswak*s to maintain oral hygiene and fresh breath for ages, but the Muslim soldiers on the outskirts of Egypt had forgotten to brush for quite a while.

Having reached this brilliant conclusion, the leader ordered his soldiers to start *miswak*-ing all at once. When the Egyptians heard that the Muslims were rubbing their teeth with dry twigs, they were petrified. They thought the soldiers were preparing to devour them alive. "Only then, my brothers, was the Muslim army able to win the battle and open the land," the imam told us.

That day, after their workout, I saw the bearded bunch

standing in front of the large mirror in the shower room. With a hair dryer in one hand and a small comb in the other, each man carefully groomed his beard while arguing about whether a Muslim woman should only wear *hijab*, or totally cover in a *burqa*.

Scene Seven

What makes the piece of cloth with which a Muslim woman covers her hair so important to her faith? I've seen Christian nuns cover similarly. But when I looked into how it all started, I read that it was the ancient Assyrians who introduced head covers to the world to distinguish married ladies from slaves and prostitutes. When the Assyrians conquered the kingdom of Israel, this tradition, along with others, was passed on to the Jews. Married Jewish women started covering too, and with the passing of time, covering became a symbol of modesty, dignity, and religiousness. A few Muslim scholars have come to a similar conclusion: they believe that the verses about *hijab* in the Koran have been misinterpreted. The scripture, in their opinion, was referring to the Prophet's wives. It demanded that they dress differently so that they could be recognized. The details of that dress code, nevertheless, are still disputable. We don't know exactly how the Prophet's wives dressed. Did they only cover their hair, or did they wear whole *burqa*s? We also don't know if that code applies to all Muslim women. Opinions are all we have.

But why would a Muslim girl in our modern world wear *hijab*? Is it true piety, or is she just doing what others are doing? When I couldn't find an answer to this question in books, I started asking some of the covered girls and women I knew. A friend of my mother's put it plainly: "For older women, covering is the most appropriate thing to do. It spares me from having to visit my hairdresser every week." Another lady in the room said, "Not only that, *hijab* improves the shape of the face and hides double chins and flabby necks."

Back when I was at university, I heard a recently covered girl talk about her experience with *hijab*. We all knew that she was in love with another student two years our senior. It was an exceptionally warm winter day, and we were waiting outside for the next lecture to begin. One of the girls asked her about covering, and she said, "Ahmed has proposed to me, but his religious family wouldn't approve of their son marrying an uncovered girl. He asked me to start wearing *hijab*, and I said okay." Most of the girls agreed that covering could increase a girl's chances of getting married these days; some said they were thinking about beginning to cover soon, themselves.

"You guys enjoy the company of us modern-looking girls. You love to hang out with us and have fun. But when it comes to marriage and commitment, you start looking for old-fashioned, conservative girls like your mothers," one of the uncovered girls said, almost spitting her words on us boys. She then turned to our covered friend and said, "Personally, I'd rather spend the rest of my life unmarried than hook a husband with a piece of cloth. It's got nothing

to do with religion. This is hypocrisy. You are all hypocrites."
She grabbed her handbag and left.

When I met some old friends a few years ago, I was
quite surprised to hear that she too had covered her hair
after marrying a religious man.

Scene Eight

Driving a car in Baghdad became an unbearable
nuisance after the war, with blocked streets, highways, and
bridges, as well as the unpredictable explosions, the U.S.
military patrols roaming the city night and day, and the
many security checkpoints that were anything but secure. A
drive that had usually taken fifteen minutes on the highway
was now taking three hours or more. I, like many other
Baghdadis, decided to drive my car only short distances to
visit friends and to shop for groceries. For long distances, we
started using taxis. They were easy to find, easy to leave, and
reasonably affordable.

I had finished my French class at the French Cultural
Center on Abu Nuwas Street one day—studying French was
a perfect distraction from the frustrating postwar reality—
and taken a taxi back home. Only a few blocks from my
house, the driver said, "Look at that whore!" I turned around
and saw a young girl walking on the opposite side of the
street. She was wearing a long, heavy, loose grey cloak that
covered most of her body. A dark grey *hijab* covered her hair
too. She was the furthest person from being a whore!

"Why did you say that?" I asked him, thinking he may

have known the girl personally, which still didn't give him the right to call her names.

"Can't you see how long the strap of her bag is? It's almost touching her vagina," he said.

I couldn't believe my ears. There was a string of prayer beads dangling from the car's rearview mirror, and small verses of the Koran decorated parts of the dashboard too. The middle-aged taxi driver was surrounding himself with reminders of religion, yet he didn't hesitate to call a poor innocent girl on the street a whore just because she was carrying a long-strapped bag. Now aside from my friend Adham's likening girls wearing *hijab* to blossoming roses, and aside from all the different interpretations of the verses that supposedly prescribe covering for women in the Koran; for many years, *hijab* supporters have been claiming that covering the hair protects girls and women from being harmed or abused, verbally or sexually. They also blame the rising incidents of rape and sexual harassment on uncovered women, who by shamelessly disobeying God's law encourage men to make sexual advances.

When I browse through my parents' old photo albums, or watch old Egyptian films on television, I'm often baffled by the fact that the women of that era—we're talking about the fifties, sixties, and seventies—hardly experienced any type of abuse while walking down the streets, or driving, or working with their male colleagues despite their uncovered coiffured—sometimes funny!—hair, made-up faces, and tight short dresses, whereas Muslim women nowadays frequently face abuse, even rape, and their several layers of covers fall short of protecting them.

CHAPTER 12

An Unfavorable Yoke

AND ONE OF HIS SIGNS IS THAT HE CREATED
SPOUSES FOR YOU FROM YOURSELVES SO THAT
YOU MAY HARBOR ONE ANOTHER, AND HE
BONDED YOU IN LOVE AND MERCY. IN THAT,
ARE SIGNS FOR THOSE WHO PONDER.

AND AMONG HIS SIGNS IS THE CREATION
OF THE HEAVENS AND THE EARTH, AND THE
VARIATIONS IN YOUR TONGUES AND COLORS.
IN THAT, INDEED ARE SIGNS FOR THE KNOWL-
EDGEABLE ONES.

(30.21,22)

This is probably the most frequently quoted Koranic text about marriage. The first verse can be found on almost all wedding invitations. It has been recited upon betrothals and before signing marriage contracts for centuries. The second one, however, is not as widely known. Most recitations would stop at the end of the first verse.

The similarity in structure and wording between the two verses struck me while I was reading the Koran one day. They both emphasize the value of pondering. In fact, the chapter Al-Roum (The Romans), in which they are mentioned respectively, calls for deep contemplation on several of God's signs and tokens, including marriage and the obvious differences between human beings.

It somehow occurred to me that God, through those verses, is sending a message that He wants different people from different races, cultures, and even faiths to interact and integrate in marriage. I know my new perception is at odds with mainstream Islamic interpretations. But I am only doing as God wants us to do: I have tried to decode His signs.

Scene One

On a starry summer night at the breezy terrace of a cozy café, we sat around a small table and watched the panoramic view of old buildings crammed together in downtown Amman like a bright, colorful rug thrown at the city hills and valleys. While my friend exhaled lemon-mint-scented smoke from his *argeeleh* (hookah), we talked about politics, religion, love, and marriage. Isa (Jesus, in Arabic) is a Catholic Christian. When we first met, he introduced himself to me by saying, "I'm a Catholic Muslim," a common joke that hints at the Christians' alignment with the prevailing culture in Jordan, as well as other predominantly Islamic countries.

A few months before that, I had written an article in support of the Christian families forced to flee their ancestral lands in Mosul, northern Iraq, as part of religious-cleansing operations there. Our mutual friend Peter forwarded my article along with my phone number in Amman to Isa. He called me; we met for coffee and talked. I don't know why, but it suddenly crossed my mind to ask Isa a question that was buzzing around in my head: "Would you approve of your sister marrying a Muslim man?"

"Absolutely not!" He answered without taking any time to think about the prospect. Apparently, I wasn't the first to ask because he had the answer on the tip of his tongue, ready to shoot. To be honest, I was slightly disappointed. I thought someone as open-minded as Isa would take a more liberal view, and my disappointment must have shown. "Don't get me wrong!" Isa said. "I know there are very good

Muslim men out there, and they might be better than many
of the Christians I know. I also know they can make very
good husbands and fathers. But it's not just about two
people getting married. It's a matter of traditions, the role
they play in our lives, and the risks involved in challenging
them."

The conventional obstacles Isa talked about couldn't
stop many young couples from taking the bold step in countries known for religious diversity like Lebanon. They flew
to adjacent Cyprus to sign civil marriage contracts. Unlike
Lebanon, laws in Cyprus allow interfaith marriages. After
a short honeymoon in the picturesque island, they'd return
to live as any other wedded couple in their own country.
This trick, unfortunately, cannot work in less-heterogeneous
Arab countries where interfaith couples face accusations of
adultery and might be sentenced to long prison terms—or
even death.

"Besides, I don't think my sister would have a secure life
with a husband who has religious and legal permission to
marry three other wives, and who can divorce her whenever
he—not she—desires," Isa said, stressing the last part. He
blew out smoke more frequently as he continued: "We live
in an extremely conservative community. Can you tell me
how an interfaith couple is supposed to lead a peaceful life
in such a resentful environment? They will be rejected by the
Muslims and the Christians. The Muslims will say, *Here is
a Muslim man who's chosen an infidel Christian instead of
a good Muslim girl to mother his children.* The Christians,
on the other hand, will scorn the girl for agreeing to marry

a Muslim against the will and consent of her family. They'll think she must have sinned with him, and her family's reputation will be tarnished forever." Isa did have a point, but I wasn't totally convinced.

Scene Two

"Every time, I come back home hating myself for getting stuck in that dreadful situation." My Syrian friend, Rana, also a Catholic, was venting her fury on the phone. Rana and I share a passion for music, and we both love the voice of the Lebanese diva Fayrouz. And through that, we have managed to build a solid friendship.

Rana sounded really upset: "Every once in a while, a Syrian Christian comes from Europe or the States to search for a good wife from home. Their mothers prepare lists of the eligible bachelorettes from among their relatives and acquaintances, and the prospective grooms spend the holiday meeting the candidates at family banquets and social events.

"It's so demeaning! I feel like I'm putting myself up for auction, desperate to be picked by the buyer. If not for my family's insistence, I swear I would never go. The worst part is when I later hear that they've chosen other girls, or even left the country without taking anyone. It totally destroys my self-esteem. I start to think, *Why didn't he choose me? There must be something wrong with me.*"

I've only known Rana for a few years, but I honestly think she's one of the most refined girls I've ever met. I tell her that all the time, but I understand and respect her agony.

It's probably because of that agony, I thought Rana might have a different opinion than Isa, so I allowed myself to ask her the same touchy question. But to my surprise, I got the very same answer: "No way!"

She told me the story of a family friend, a Syrian Christian lady who'd dared to cross the red line somewhere in the sixties. She fell in love with a Muslim boy, but they knew too well that their relationship was destined to fall apart. They decided to run away, get married, and live beyond the reach of their families and tribes. Rana told me that she never got to meet the escapee woman in person, but she saw some of her old pictures and spoke to her sister. The family woke up one day and found that their girl had disappeared. They looked everywhere but she was gone. The woman's sister who told Rana the story was engaged to a young Christian man from the same village. When the scandal broke and his family heard that her sister had run away with a Muslim boy, they forced their son to end the engagement. No man has proposed to her since.

Her heartbroken father couldn't bear to live in disgrace. People insulted him and spat on his sons when they saw them walk in the village. His brothers urged him to send someone to track and kill the sinner and restore the family's bruised honor, but the old man loved his daughter so much that he couldn't stand the thought of killing her. Instead, he sold his property and left the village to reside in the capital with his wife, sons, and daughter. Damascus, a vast city where no one knew about their shame, seemed like a perfect choice for the family, but the father never stopped grieving over his daughter until a stroke left him paralyzed for the rest of his life. To this day, no one knows anything about the girl. Her brothers and sister still blame her for all the hardships that have befallen them since the day she decided to run away to marry a Muslim.

"But life has changed so much since that time," I told Rana. Girls are more independent now. I've heard stories about Syrian interfaith couples that have had the courage to stand their ground against all odds.

"Yes, there are a few cases, but they are the exception to the rule. The thing is, more and more Christian men are migrating to the West for better job opportunities, permanent residence, and citizenship. Most of them marry Western girls there. The men who can't afford to leave can barely make enough money to maintain themselves. They don't even think about marriage," Rana said. "It's a very bad time for us Christian girls in this country."

Scene Three

I always thought of cross pendants as a symbol of faith, but Isa surprised me again: "They are, but that's not the only reason why single Christian girls wear them. It's also a way of letting the Christian men, interested in marriage, know that they are available. And eligible." When I asked Rana about it, she said teasingly, "True, and it's our way of telling the Muslim men to save themselves the trouble." I thought this was interesting. Maybe Muslim girls living in the West wore pendants with Allah's name inscribed on them or wrapped their hair with scarves for the same purpose. I remember when I fell in love with a Christian girl during my adolescence, her cross was never an obstacle to our relationship. Well, maybe it would have been, had we planned on marrying.

A conservative society may tolerate interfaith love as long as it's kept in the dark. It sometimes happens that while waiting for Mr. Right to knock on the door, some girls—Muslims and Christians—can't help falling in love with Mr. Wrong. Once the lovers have decided to step into the light and give legitimacy to their relationship, it drives people crazy. Back when I was at university, gossip spread about a love story between a Muslim student and a Christian girl of Armenian descent. Thousands of Armenian families had fled persecution under the Ottoman Empire during the early twentieth century and come a long way to live and settle in several Arab countries, including Iraq, where they were permitted to work, study, and build churches. Over the years, they and their children and grandchildren all became naturalized citizens. My brothers and I have several Armenian friends, and it's quite an irony that many of them—despite the fact that they spoke Armenian at home and went to Armenian churches regularly—have never set foot in Armenia. Iraq is the only homeland they know.

Right from the beginning, the Sunni Muslim boy and Orthodox Armenian girl were keen to declare their relationship. Everyone knew about their love, including their parents. They both came from well-educated, upper-middle-class families who lived a liberal lifestyle (maybe not liberal enough to stomach an interfaith marriage!). The boy frequently visited his lover at home and took her out to dinner in restaurants where they acted like any other engaged couple. This went on for several years until one Christmas when the boy's mother bought the girl a gold cross necklace. In her own subtle way, she wanted to remind the two of them of the risk they were taking by brazenly challenging the social norms.

The girl's family decided to send her on a long vacation to the United States, where her elder brother lived. Once she got there, they pushed her to find a job and apply for residence. After a couple of years, she got married to an Armenian American. When the shocking news reached her lover in Baghdad, he immediately threw himself into a new relationship—with a Sunni Muslim girl. His family welcomed the news. He proposed to the girl, and they got married in a short time. And that was the end of yet another big love story.

Scene Four

The law in Iraq allows Christian or Jewish wives of Muslim men to keep their original faiths after marriage. I've had Muslim friends in school whose mothers were European Christians, and a number of my father's friends are married to Christian ladies from different parts of the world too. This acceptance of non-Muslim spouses, nevertheless, is not unconditional and is somehow discriminatory. Most Arab courts, if not all, would not process applications for mixed marriages between Muslim women and non-Muslim men unless the husbands-to-be convert to Islam first, according to Sharia.

"He's not a true Muslim—he only converted to marry a Muslim girl," some people still grumble. I've always wondered about what makes one man a true Muslim and another not. Which of the two am I? Does an oral profession that there is only One God and that Mohammed is His sent messenger suffice to deem someone a true Muslim? If so, then why aren't people happy with their daughters marrying new converts? They are Muslims too, aren't they? Does a true Muslim have to be the child of Muslim parents? And what about true Christians? Is anyone baptized into Christ a true Christian? Is every child born to a Jewish mother a devout Jew? Can we define a Muslim man as a male who doesn't drink alcohol or eat pork and has a circumcised penis?

There are non-Muslim men who'd go as far as to bear the pain of adult circumcision just to be able to marry the Muslim girls they love. They also don't mind changing their faith and names for that purpose. But is that enough? I don't think there will ever be a way to find out who is "true" and who is not. Our looks, spoken words, and visible deeds can make an impact on others, but they're just the tip of the iceberg.

I thought about that when I heard that an Iraqi Muslim girl was going to marry an Indian Sikh. They'd fallen in love while working together at a grand hotel in Baghdad. The news of their marriage left everyone dumbfounded. Despite some similarities between the two religions, Muslims consider Sikhs to be unbelievers. There is no way a Muslim girl can marry a Sikh man unless he becomes Muslim too. The man agreed to convert, and they did marry, but they kept facing such enormous pressure that they finally decided to leave Iraq to start a new and less hectic life in India. Legally and religiously, the couple didn't do anything wrong to deserve execration; their marriage was one hundred percent valid. But it wasn't really about religion as much as it was about pride. Arab men can't tolerate strangers trespassing on their property. And in mixed marriages, Muslim girls are treated as plundered belongings. Losing them to strangers shames their entire clan.

Scene Five

Two Iraqi girls I know very well got married at almost the same time. One of them married a Muslim man in Baghdad. The other, after a long struggle with her family, married an Englishman in London. Most of the people I know were expecting the first marriage to thrive and the second to crash. In less than one year, the first marriage was obviously falling apart. The wife had to fight a tough battle in court before she finally got divorced. But that was not the end of her tribulations. The Muslim ex-husband felt his pride had been wounded. He dedicated his time, effort, and money to destroying the lives of his ex-wife and her family.

When the other girl finally convinced her parents to give her permission to marry the man of her choice, he still had to take the necessary step before signing the marriage contract. The groom went to the local mosque and changed his religion from Christianity to Islam. They have been married for more than ten years, and they have three children. The convert Englishman has proved to be both a good spouse and a good father. Of course, there are numerous instances of mixed marriages that have ended in divorce, just as there are millions of happily married Muslim couples. Marriage has always been a fifty-fifty chance. And except for affection and respect, there is no guarantee for a couple's happiness: not their religion, not their families, not anything.

Scene Six

My friend Omar's parents are an unusual couple, a Muslim man married to a native Christian woman, who continued living inside the country with their sons. Omar's father had first met his mother when he was a young physician at the hospital where she worked as a nurse. Her Christian family was poor, and pride was not among their priorities in life. They were fascinated by the fact that their daughter was marrying a handsome, ambitious doctor.

The couple's two sons grew up as Muslims—non-practicing, though. Their parents led a modern, secular life like most middle-class Iraqis then. Omar received a fine education, and when he graduated from university, his family thought it was time he proposed to the girl he loved. The parents of the girl whom Omar had planned to marry saw things differently: they thought marrying their daughter off to a man whose mother was Christian could shame the family name. "He's only half a Muslim," they said.

Back then, Iraq was at war with Iran. Omar managed to get a scholarship to continue his studies abroad, a precious chance to escape death on the battlefield. Leaving behind the great love of his life, Omar packed his bags and left Iraq with a broken heart. He later married a British girl, and his wife (just like his mother) decided to keep her original faith; his children (just like him and his brother) are now Muslims with Islamic first names and surnames. Will they too face rejection if they want to marry Muslim girls one day? It may be a bit early to ask this question. The girl Omar had loved and proposed to never get married. Her parents died years ago, and she has since been living alone in their house.

Scene Seven

Just before boarding the Qatar Airways jet in Kuala Lumpur, a middle-aged Malay man started a conversation with me. Bekr worked for a multinational oil company in Doha. He was going back to work after a short vacation with his family in Malaysia.

"I wonder if it's permissible to pray while seated in the plane. It keeps changing direction, and it's almost impossible to kneel and prostrate in such a narrow space," he said after giving me his business card.

I had already met many Muslim Malaysians and was familiar with their questions about Sharia. They are often under the misconception that all Arabs are religiously knowledgeable and qualified to answer their queries, no matter how specific they might be.

"Why don't you wait until you've reached Doha, taken a shower, and had some rest? And then you can pray," I suggested.

He didn't look convinced, and drifted to another topic: "My colleagues at work told me that in the Arab world a Muslim man can marry a Christian woman without her having to convert to Islam first. Do you have that in Iraq too?"

"Yes, we actually do, and they can keep practicing their faith after marriage." However, Christian women married to Muslim men in Iraq—as well as in many other Islamic countries—can't, for instance, stop their husbands from taking other wives, if so they wished. Nor can their daughters have shares of inheritance equal to their brothers' because they have Christian mothers. No, in cases like these, Islamic law has the final say.

Bekr seemed confused about my answer and told me that in his country, courts don't give permission to Muslims willing to marry non-Muslim wives—be they Christians, Jews, Buddhists, or Hindus—because they are all infidels. They are required to prove that they've changed their religion to Islam before marrying Muslim men. It was now my turn to be confused.

The Prophet himself married a Christian: Maria the Egyptian, also known as Maria the Copt, was Mohammed's wife and the mother of his deceased infant child Ibrahim. He also married Safiyya bint Huyayy, a Jew from Medina.

"So why can't we do the same?" I asked Bekr. "There is not one verse in the Koran that says Muslims are allowed to marry nonbelievers. And the Prophet—peace be upon him—only married Maria and Safiyya after they'd become Muslims." I actually didn't know that. I thought they'd converted to Islam after marrying Mohammed. When I searched in Islamic history books, it turned out Bekr's statement was accurate.

On the verge of another shift of discussion, I wanted to remind Bekr that the Koran differentiates between two types of non-Muslims, and that both Christians and Jews are our fellow believers in the One God. But the gate was open, and we had to get moving.

Months later, I found interesting information online about marriages that had taken place in Andalusia between Muslim women and Christian men during the Arab rule of the Iberian Peninsula many centuries ago. Relying on the Koran's recognition of the Christians as equal believers in God, the Christian husbands had been allowed to keep their birth faith. Such cases were very rare, but there is no denying that they occurred. I remembered my discussion with Bekr at the Kuala Lumpur airport and thought of sending him an email. I searched for his business card but it must have fallen out of my wallet. I wonder what he'd say about those Andalusian couples.

Scene Eight

"A Muslim husband is obliged to respect his wife's faith, whereas a Christian or Jewish husband might insult his Muslim wife's religion, or even prevent her from practicing it, for they don't acknowledge Islam as a true religion in the first place," one of my friends said. His justification didn't convince me because it was one assumption built on another. First, women today are not blindly compliant, and they can't be forced to keep or dump their faith unless they themselves want to do so. Second, if a non-Muslim husband tries to abuse his Muslim wife, she can walk out of marriage and ask for divorce, and she will be awarded alimony. It's her legal right.

When I researched what the Bible and the Torah have to say about interfaith marriages, I stumbled upon some very stern warnings: *Do not be yoked together with unbelievers. For what do righteousness and wickedness have in common? Or what fellowship can light have with darkness?* (2 Corinthians 6:14). And while browsing the Book of Exodus in the Torah, I found: *And when you take wives from among their daughters for your sons, their daughters will lust after their gods and will cause your sons to lust after their gods* (34:16). Although that sounds familiar, there is one big difference: both the Bible and the Torah have long ceased to dictate laws in many parts of the world. In our part of the world, the Koran hasn't.

In Islam, acceptance and announcement are essential for validating any marriage. The man must make a proposal, and when the woman gives consent, the marriage will be considered valid. It also should be made known to everyone that the sane, adult couple has agreed to take both social and legal responsibility for their commitment. These prerequisites are meant to preserve the integrity of society, and they generally do. I just don't understand why interfaith marriages—as long as they meet the acceptance and announcement condition—are strongly frowned upon.

What about the children? I have pious friends whose

parents are anything but religious. I have other friends who don't believe in God despite having grown up in devout Muslim families. I've also seen them trade places. Our parents can affect our spiritual choices in life when we are children. But so can our friends, the books that we read, the films we watch, and the experiences we have. We can't prevent children from making friends, going to school, reading books, or watching television. By the same logic, I don't think there is any point in banning interfaith marriages for fear they could confuse the sons' and daughters' religion. If anything, they would make children choose for themselves which religion they want to follow, which cannot be a bad thing. After all, God says in the Koran that a man's faith is his own choice, not his parents'.

Getting married is probably the most difficult decision a man or a woman will ever make. I can list a dozen good reasons to remain single. Most of us have enough burdens on our shoulders already, and the last thing we need to do is add more responsibilities to them. It's really sad when interfaith couples decide to rise to the challenge but face discrimination and are sometimes forced to run away from their families and hometowns. Nature has always allowed different species to coexist, mate, and reproduce. Hybrids are everywhere. If we humans are a part of nature, why can't we be more like it?

CHAPTER 13

Hadith

AND MOHAMMED IS BUT A MESSENGER,
BEFORE WHOM THE OTHER MESSENGERS
HAVE ALL PASSED AWAY. WHETHER THEN HE
DIES OR IS SLAIN, WILL YOU TURN ON YOUR
HEELS? HE, WHO TURNS ON HIS HEELS, WILL
NOT HARM GOD IN ANY WAY. AND GOD WILL
RECOMPENSE THE BEHOLDEN.

(3.144)

When I started writing this book, I didn't have a clear agenda in mind other than to talk about how religion was permeating every aspect of my life and creating confusion. I had so much to say about *hadith*, or the sayings of Mohammed as told by his contemporaries, but I thought it would be better to leave them till the end. After a couple of pages, I realized it wasn't even an option. The Prophet's sayings and teachings have forced their way into almost every single chapter. I couldn't ignore them while writing about Muslim women's rights, or the influence of traditions in a Muslim society, or about conversion, or mosques, or food, or headscarves, or even sex.

Scene One

The Odd Couple aired every Friday afternoon. My brother (five years my senior) and I used to watch it on television while having lunch in the living room. I was ten then, not so fluent in English, so I had to read the Arabic subtitles, and so did my brother. We munched on crispy chicken drumsticks and giggled at the funny situations taking place in the New York apartment where Jack Lemmon and Walter Matthau—Felix and Oscar in the show—lived. Both my brother and I were too young to notice that the show's title couldn't have suited the two of us better. Indeed, we were, and still are, the odd siblings.

We spent our childhood years fighting over anything and everything, and we used to give our poor mother such a hard time that she covered her face with her hands and cried after every battle between us. It always started with a small quarrel that would quickly escalate into a vicious argument. At that point, it was impossible to stop before one of us was totally defeated. Except for our surname—and the few television series we loved to watch together—my brother and I hardly had anything in common. These differences only deepened as we grew older, but we reached an unspoken agreement to put an end to our fights. Since there wasn't much we could do to change our biological kinship, we had no choice but to accept each other, or at least to try.

When my brother decided to leave Iraq, I drove him to the station where he would take the bus to Jordan. We kept silent all the way. Surprisingly, and despite our notorious history, we had an embarrassingly emotional farewell at the station. We cried our eyes out as we hugged goodbye, and peace finally prevailed. Today, after almost twenty years from that historical moment, we are still poles apart. But whenever we meet and a dispute arises—which is likely— one or both of us will try changing the subject; otherwise, one will just pretend to have something else to do and walk out of the room quietly.

My brother turned religious many years ago. He now prays and fasts; he doesn't take any interest on his bank savings because that would be usury, strictly forbidden in Islam. And of course, he went on a pilgrimage to Mecca. My brother's religiosity, nevertheless, hasn't helped bridge the gap between us. Actually, it may have widened it. Three years ago, during the month of Ramadan, our family gath- ered on the weekend to break our fast together. While waiting for the sun to set, we sat in the living room to watch a live broadcast of prayer from Saudi Arabia on television. Millions of men and women had come from all over the world to visit and pray at the most sacred place for Muslims. The camera showed their faces while they prayed in humility facing the Ka'ba.

"What's this man doing? Is he crazy?" my brother asked suddenly.

I was busy reading something, but as I looked at the screen, I saw a young man praying. Nothing extraordinary.

"What's wrong?" I asked.

"Didn't you see him? He was looking at the sky during prayer," my brother exclaimed.

"And what's wrong with that?" I asked again.

"Don't you know that Muslims should lower their gaze while praying?" he said in a stern, authoritarian tone of voice I knew too well. It used to get on my nerves and evoke the rebel in me when we were kids. "His prayer will not be accepted. It's void. He will need to start anew after they finish."

"And where in the Koran does God say that?" I couldn't help asking.

He shook his head at the naïvety of my question and told me that not all technical details of our rituals are mentioned in the Koran. The Prophet had later taught many of them.

"But isn't it possible that those details, or at least some of them—orally transferred for centuries before they were finally transcribed—may have been taken out of context?"

My brother's face turned red. The veins on his forehead were pulsating with anger. "Are you suggesting that we should not comply with God's clear commands to follow the teachings of Prophet Mohammed?"

I had asked myself this question numerous times already. "I didn't say that," I replied. "But what if a certain teaching contradicts common sense? I mean, here we have this man—who probably came a long way to pray at the Sacred Mosque in Mecca—who looked at the sky while he was praying. And now you are saying he's made a big mistake and that his prayer is not valid?"

Afraid that our hard-earned truce might be in jeopardy, our parents warily listened to our discussion. My brother was on the verge of erupting, but I debated the issue because I could relate to the praying man. I have been there too.

Right after I'd finished praying in the mosque one Friday in Baghdad, and as we shook hands, preparing to leave, one of my neighbors gripped my arm and said, "Listen brother, I've been watching you while you prayed. You've made a big mistake. You laid your arms on the floor when you prostrated. Don't you know that only the palms are supposed to touch the floor?"

"No, I don't know that," I replied, still not fathoming why he was so concerned about something as minor as placing my arm or hand on the floor.

"Well, now that you do, you'd better start redeeming the years you spent praying the wrong way. If you want, you can go back to the *hadith* books and read the Prophet's teachings on this particularity."

Indeed. I checked and was startled by the many other things we were supposed to steer clear of during prayer: yawning, having scrumptious food in the room, closing the eyes (because that's an imitation of Jewish prayer), having fire lit before a worshipper (a loathsome Magian tradition), reflecting on worldly issues, passing in front of a praying man, rolling up one's sleeves, rubbing stones, cracking the fingers, stroking the beard, and turning the head or the body to the sides, just to name a few, are all forbidden, *haram*. But that was not all. The most bizarre was avoiding clapping in prayer. I couldn't believe my eyes when I read it. Why would people need to clap while they pray? Some imams allowed clapping for women and banned it for men, while others tolerated a few faint claps in case a man or a woman wanted to notify a caller that they couldn't answer his call, the books said. But how often did we actually need to do that, and how important were such technicalities that they needed to be discussed so thoroughly? I felt lost in a maze of contradictory, trivial opinions.

"You might as well be one of those New Age Muslims who are remolding religion to their liking and creating an Islam of their own, taking bits from the Koran and others from the Christian Bible or the Jewish Torah, some ancient wisdom from pagan faiths with modern secular values. And by doing so, they think they are being true Muslims," my brother's voice, cynical this time, interrupted my recollection and brought my attention back to the wrestling mat.

"That's exactly what I'm saying. Maybe it is time to go over all those teachings and apply logic and rational thinking to them."

My brother's jaw dropped, but he tried to remain calm: "If I can't change your opinion, I can at least warn you of God's wrath. We are all going to die someday, and you need to keep that in mind. Try to save your soul from eternal torture in hell before it's too late!"

Having hit a brick wall, there was nothing more for us to say. Besides, our parents had endured enough tension already, and it was time to break fasting anyway. We went to perform the sunset prayer.

Scene Two

An American friend online wrote me this:

You guys say today's Bible is not authentic. You don't

believe it's the genuine word of God, but rather a distorted version of it. Through the centuries, you insist, the Bible has been rewritten several times. Let me tell you, this is true. It's a historically known fact that several canons in Christianity had been drawn up by the Ecumenical Councils many years after the crucifixion. But could you please explain to me how is it even conceivable that today's Koran is the same book uttered by Mohammed over fourteen centuries ago? You really believe that not a single word has been changed? Oh, please!

It wasn't my first time being asked that question, so I was neither surprised nor offended by it. Many of the Westerners I've met online or in person have raised suspicions about the accuracy of the Muslim scripture. In fact, there are many Muslims who have similar doubts but are afraid or ashamed to admit them. I know that because at a certain point in my life I had them too. "The Koran was Mohammed's only miracle," I've heard scholars say. Unlike Jesus, the Prophet didn't bring the dead back to life, heal the blind, or walk on water. He was only given the Koran. And through the Koran, he was able to transform an entire nation religiously, socially, and politically.

In the chapter of Al-Qiyama (The Resurrection), God tells Mohammed that he needn't worry about compiling the verses of the book, for He Himself will see that they are properly collected and recited. This is what the Koran says. But do I believe the book I have in my room is exactly the same one read by the early Muslims fourteen centuries ago? I know what I'm going to say may sound strange or even absurd: yes, in my heart of hearts, I do believe that

God has kept His promise. Cryptic, beautifully rhythmic, and rhymed, I don't think the Koran could have been the creation of man, let alone an illiterate man. It's so deep and complex that I often need to use the Tafseer or interpretation books to help me sort out some of its intricate meanings. All Tafseers are dependent on the Prophet's sayings, *hadith*.

It is practically impossible to navigate through what was happening at the time of the revelation of the Koran or understand the way the new religion was reshaping people's lives without going back to *hadith*. The Muslims started quoting the Prophet immediately after his death in the early seventh century. Contradictory narrations, however, were soon detected, and they started to cause controversy. There arose an urgent necessity for a system of scrutiny to distinguish between genuine and false sayings. What we know today as the Science of *Hadith* has evolved over the years from an oral method of tracking the roots of narratives and the chains of narrators to a well-documented and archived mechanism. It has proved to be very useful in filtering thousands of alleged sayings, but it can't resolve the confusion completely. At least not to me.

Scene Three

My first impression of the supervising officer at the military unit where I was assigned to serve after graduation from university was that he must have been strictly religious. The slim, grim-faced civil engineer from northern Iraq, looking somewhere in his late thirties, scarcely missed a prayer in the mosque. With every call to prayer, he performed ablutions and hurried to the next-door mosque accompanied by lower-ranking officers and a number of my colleagues. Out of boredom, I decided to join them one day, and I actually liked it. Before long, I became a prominent member of the devotees' club. A part of me—my niggling conscience, perhaps—was not so happy with this arrangement, though. Was I feigning piety to please the officer and get benefits? Was I manipulating God?

Weighed down by guilt, I began to skip the afternoon prayers at the mosque. Nevertheless, I kept praying at home, and occasionally at our neighborhood mosques on Fridays. I knew that praying with fellow believers at the mosque was preferable to praying solo at home. And in an ancient Muslim city like Baghdad, there was an abundance of mosques everywhere. Their minarets and domes rose high in every district, but the hectic pace of modern life has left many of them redundant except on Fridays, during Ramadan, and on a number of other Islamic occasions. Other than that, only a few men and women, mainly elderly, committed to praying in them during the week. Many of the practicing Muslims I know pray in their homes. And I have several friends who don't pray at all.

When the officer noticed my absence, he sent one of my colleagues to check on me. As if playing tug-of-war, my colleague was pulling my arm, dragging me to join the march to the mosque. I held tight to my desk like a stubborn child and refused to move.

"Oh come on, Ali! Your damn devil is so strong, don't let him control you!" He said through gritted teeth, pulling my arm so hard that it actually hurt.

"I'm not going with you. I will pray when I go back home." I tried to make it clear to him in the friendliest possible way. And it worked: he finally let go of my arm.

Adopting a different strategy, he asked me, "Don't you know what the Prophet, peace be upon him, said about the Muslims who pray in their houses instead of going to the mosque?"

It was my first time hearing this saying. But now that I was categorized as a pray-at-home Muslim, I was curious to know.

"*Indeed I was about to have my men fetch me bunches of firewood, and then walk to the people who were praying in their houses with no excuse, and have them and their houses burned down.*"

I couldn't hide my resentment when my colleague finished the quote, and I thought, *Am I supposed to believe this?* Mohammed endured so much pain, pain that no other mortal could have endured, and yet he was able to forsake vengeance. He even forgave the slayers of his beloved uncle Hamza, whose dead body was brutally mutilated. They ripped it open and ate his raw liver, but Mohammed forgave them all and set them free. He inculcated his followers with the concept that forgiveness was no less generous an act than the paying of alms. Why would he want to burn Muslim men, women, and children whose only crime was praying to God in their homes?

Another of the Prophet's sayings that I had read a long time before strictly implied that no one but God had the right to punish with fire. Which of the two contradictory sayings was I supposed to believe? One of them made perfect sense to me; the other made no sense at all, and I just couldn't buy it... but what if someone else did? What if some desperate young man decided to burn his family or his neighbors to death because they weren't praying at the mosque? With the current rise of religious fanaticism among young people, this frightening prospect isn't as farfetched as many of us would like to think.

"I'm sorry, but this *hadith* can't be true," I told my zealous colleague.

Having wasted so much time on a hopeless case like me, he sighed, shrugged, and then hastened to catch the prayer at the mosque.

Scene Four

I had already made up my mind that I wasn't going to weddings anymore when I received the invitation to Saeed's. I'd had very bad experiences with wedding parties. Every time, I ended up sitting silent and uncomfortable in my suit, watching people dance like idiots until dinner was served. Because of the deafening music, it wasn't possible to have a decent conversation with the other guests at the table. And every time, I got a terrible headache that lasted several days. One night after returning home, I decided to quit all weddings. But it was hard to turn down Saeed's invitation.

My longtime friend has always been extremely polite. I don't remember him ever fighting in school, maybe not in his entire life. He graduated from medical college with high distinction and specialized in bone surgery. His bride-to-be was a religious girl from a religious family. They were going to live with his religious parents. Hence, the wedding ceremony was going to be conducted according to Islamic traditions. I had never been to an Islamic wedding before, and I was curious; besides, I would have been embarrassed to decline the invitation, so I decided to give it a go.

First and foremost, I knew it was going to be a manly event. And indeed it was. The groom's male friends and relatives arrived at his family house before sunset prayer. When the call to prayer reverberated from the adjacent mosque, we all walked to pray there. I had no complaints so far. In fact, I thought it was far less annoying than the other weddings I had attended before. When we went back to Saeed's house after prayer, all the rooms had been cleared of furniture and filled with rows of plastic chairs. We took our seats and waited for the show to begin. According to one of the Prophet's sayings, Muslims should declare their marriages by throwing banquets for relatives and friends, and beating drums on the occasion. A group of four bearded men holding large round drums walked into the room and started chanting praises to Allah and the Prophet.

All of a sudden, we heard ululations coming from the room where the women had gathered to celebrate. While they were very typical of traditional Iraqi weddings, I was a bit surprised to hear them at Saeed's. According to another *hadith*, loud female voices are not supposed to be heard in public. I guess it was one of those instances where customs dared to defy religion and could still get away with it. The men in our room sent one of the children to remind the women to keep their voices low. After a few songs, it was time for dinner. The piles of steaming food laid out on a long buffet in the garden were the second reminder of the women's contribution to the night. It was also a good chance to meet and chat with some old friends.

Fueled by good, spicy food, the band struck their drums louder to some very different lyrics after dinner. I still remember one of the songs: "Tonight while I savor pleasure with my beloved one, my single friends will be tossing and turning in their beds of burning desire." One of the singers winked to Saeed, who smiled, lowered his eyes, and blushed.

When the show was over, we queued to shake hands with the groom and the males of his family, wishing the couple happiness and blessed offspring. I couldn't sleep that night and spent long hours tossing and turning in my bed... not from sexual deprivation, but from a pounding headache because of the loud drums.

Scene Five

The chubby, grey-bearded sheikh scribbled something on a paper. He only had time to answer a few of the many questions he received every week on his popular television show.

"*Alsalamu alaikum*. I'm a Muslim woman and I've been wearing *hijab* for many years. I would like to ask the respected sheikh whether I should keep my scarf on while the maid is in the room with me, knowing that she's not a Muslim. My maid is a Christian Filipina. Thank you."

I was baffled by the caller's question. All my life I

thought Muslim women only had to cover in the presence of male strangers. Not even the most extremist clerics had prescribed covering for women in front of women. I wanted to know what the sheikh was going to say about that, but he went on taking more phone calls:

"Is it okay to listen to music, and are Muslims permitted to sing?"

"Are women allowed to go out shopping and bargain with vendors in the market?"

"Is it a sin to wax my eyebrows, and what does Islam say about tattoos?"

"My wife and I were fasting Ramadan, but we couldn't help kissing. I got aroused after a while—did that spoil my fast?"

"I have some money in a bank account, but I don't know what to do with the interest they've paid me. Shall I keep the money to myself, donate it to charity, or refuse to receive it?"

"Can I slaughter a sheep on behalf of my deceased father on Eid? I also pray for him. Will he be able to hear my prayer?"

"Are Shias considered Muslims just like us Sunnis or are they *kafirs*? Can we marry their women?"

These are examples of the types of questions people were eager to have answered on the sheikh's show and many other Islamic shows on television.

Every time I held the remote control and started flipping through channels, I saw bearded men and veiled women preaching. Thanks to modern technology, hundreds of Arabic-satellite channels are now transmitting round the clock, and most have weekly, sometimes daily, Islamic Q&A programs. There are also dozens of specialized channels entirely dedicated to Koran recitations and interpretations, Sharia law, and *hadith*. It's actually a booming business nowadays. Millions of Muslims wish to live their lives the way the Prophet had lived his, and as I said earlier, the only access we have to that era is through *hadith* books.

I can understand the Muslims' desire to promote their faith and attract new followers. Many Christian churches— Orthodox, Catholic, and Protestant—are trying to do the same thing. Their missionary satellite channels have been targeting Muslim audiences in the Arab world for some time now. I'd seen one or two of them while channel flicking. This, however, is not the aim of the numerous Islamic channels that debate historical and jurisprudential issues. They don't seem to care about converting non-Muslims, and I don't know why there are so many of them.

Another thing I don't understand is why many Muslims feel such a strong need to be guided by clergymen throughout the most intimate details of their lives. As if they will have all the right answers! What, for instance, made the caller in the *fatwa* show assume the sheikh would know about eyebrows and tattoos? I couldn't help laughing at her silly question, and I expected him to reproach her for asking it. Obviously, the man wasn't a beautician. The sheikh didn't laugh, though. He took her very seriously and tried to give her a precise answer based on yet another saying of the Prophet.

Islamic attire, food, songs, toothpaste, schools, and banks are all in very high demand these days. I've even found bottles of Islamic non-alcoholic beer while shopping at the neighborhood supermarket. It was selling exceptionally well too. Prophetic medicine, dream interpretations in accordance with Islam, using the Koran to exorcise evil demons and genies, creative ways to wrap *hijab*, and of course, *fatwa*s about anything and everything are all regular features in today's television programs, newspapers, and magazines. Every time I visit a bookstore, I see customers buying Islamic books. They make the bestseller lists everywhere whilst piles of contemporary literature books sit untouched on the shelves. But this obsession with everything prophetic and Islamic is not always completely safe. Many patients are rushed to hospitals after receiving prophetic treatments for their ailments. Several have lost their lives.

I was paging through a Saudi magazine one day and came across the dream interpretation column. *I saw our Christian neighbor – a very kind lady we all admire – visiting our house, smiling and carrying a bag of fresh fruits*, a reader inquired about the meaning of her dream. The sheikh replied, *My dear daughter, I'm afraid your dream has a bad connotation. As you may know, the Christians are infidels. They don't believe in the One God as we Muslims do. The fresh fruits your neighbor brought into your house stand for a hard time you are likely to face soon. I pray that your ultimate faith in Allah will help you get over it.* The man was pushing the reader to cut her good neighbor off because of a stupid dream! I couldn't understand why the editor had allowed something so awful to be published. Pissed off, I sent an email to the magazine, urging them to print an apology, or at least a correction. But just as I expected, nothing of the sort happened.

Scene Six

Fatwas ceased to surprise me after the infamous 2007 decree that stole the limelight from its controversial predecessors. In an attempt to solve the predicament of mixing between male and female colleagues, Dr. Ezzat Attiya—Head of the Hadith Department at the prestigious Al-Azhar University in Cairo—came up with something disgusting, obscene, despicable, and sacrilegious all at the same time. Working women, according to Attiya's fatwa, should render themselves unmarriageable by breast-feeding their male coworkers five fulfilling times. Only then will they be permitted to work together in one office. The edict immediately sparked an uproar in the media all over the world. Dr. Ezzat, relenting to massive public and government pressure, quickly withdrew his fatwa and apologized to the millions of Muslim women who worked side by side with men. He also took full responsibility for misinterpreting a particular incident mentioned in several hadith books.

But the controversy didn't stop there; it snowballed. Three years later, Sheikh Abdul Mohsin Al Obeikan—an official adviser to the Royal Court and consultant to the Ministry of Justice in Saudi Arabia—appeared on national television, commenting on Attiya's fatwa and announcing that the only way to avoid violating the strict Islamic law

ALI SHAKIR

forbidding mixing between the sexes, especially within families that hired foreign servants and drivers, would be to create a new status for those males in the household by making the wife feed them with her milk five times. This way, Al Obeikan insisted, they will be like mother and son, so the employee can mix with the females of the family without breaching the teachings of Islam that regard breast-milk kinship as an equivalent to blood relationship. The recipient, however, should not suckle milk from the woman's breast, but rather have it pumped out and given to him in a glass.

However, that's not what a third sheikh, Abi Ishaq Al Huwairi, suggested in yet another controversial *fatwa*. In order to rule out the prospect of them having sex, a man has to drink milk directly from a woman's breast. Serving the milk in a cup or a glass, Al Huwairi argued, would not achieve the purpose of the process.

The three sheikhs all claimed to have derived their obnoxious edicts from a historical occurrence mentioned in certified *hadith* books. After adoption was banned in Islam, a woman came to the Prophet to inquire about the status of her adopted child who was by then a young man. *Hadith* books say the Prophet told the woman to go back and breast-feed her adopted son so that he could remain in the family. Whether or not the young man suckled milk from her breast or drank it from a cup, we don't know.

When I was in Jordan, I went to watch an Egyptian comedy about the flood of breast-feeding *fatwas*. The actors stood in a long line in front of a gorgeous female colleague, anxiously waiting for their turn to be nurtured, frustrating the other girls in the office who didn't look as sexy. The audience was rolling in their seats at the hilarious sketch. It really makes no sense to think that a few sips of a woman's fresh breast milk could make a man—or the woman, for that matter—behave. These *fatwa*s brimmed with paradox and had all the necessary elements to make an exemplary comedy. A black comedy.

On Fatwas and Muftis

In 1989, Ayatollah Khomeini issued one of the most famous *fatwa*s of modern times against Indian-born novelist Salman Rushdie over the "blasphemous" content of the latter's book *The Satanic Verses*. The death edict forced Rushdie to spend years in deep hiding. Contrary to Khomeini's intent, his *fatwa* contributed to the success of Rushdie's book, especially among Western readers. Khomeini died a few months after announcing his decree, but it was reaffirmed by other top Iranian clerics, and it is still in effect to this day.

The notorious head of Al Qaeda signed another infamous *fatwa* in 1998. Osama bin Laden, among other Jihadis, issued a ruling to kill Americans and their allies—civilians and military alike—wherever in the world they may be for the injustice they'd done to Islam and Muslims. The *fatwa* is believed to have authorized the horrible attacks of September 11, 2001. In retaliation, George W. Bush, then President of the United States of America, initiated the

War on Terror and launched a series of military operations in Afghanistan and Iraq.

When I researched the historical roots of *fatwa*s, I learned that they were inseparably interwoven with *hadith*. In order to be validated, all *fatwa*s must be based on one or more of the Prophet's sayings. Conversely, though, it wasn't until the sixteenth-century Ottoman Empire that *fatwa*s as we know them today started to appear and their influence manifest itself. Some historians even suggest that the Turks—influenced by the heritage of the Byzantines—were the first to invent the position of the Grand Mufti in Islam. According to Professor Martin Houtsma: "The organization of the *ulama* of the Ottoman empire under a religious chief may be in some way influenced by that of the Christian hierarchy in the empire under the Ecumenical patriarch." This may not be far from the truth because Islam had long denied any sort of clerical hierarchy, especially in its early ages. All an imam was supposed to do at that time was lead prayers at the mosque, nothing more.

Muslims' need for spiritual, political, and social guidance emerged soon after the Prophet's death. His absence had created a void that was impossible for any of his disciples to fill because Mohammed wasn't only a messenger, but also a political leader, lawmaker, and military commander. For many Muslims, the hitherto fixed notion of rejecting mediators between man and God was starting to prove impractically romantic. New problems were arising and people wanted someone to tell them how the Prophet would have reacted, someone to ascertain what was right and what was wrong. There is no denying that the first caliphs were quite innovative, which leads to the discussion of another predicament. Entrusting so much power to a single individual could very likely result in dictatorship and oppression in the name of religion, a common occurrence in the history of Islam and the other religions too.

The later caliphs, nevertheless, lacked the flexibility of their predecessors and resorted to having someone else to take responsibility and blame in their stead. Several Islamist guerillas and militias nowadays have private *mufti*s to facilitate their killings. Al Qaeda alone has several provincial *mufti*s in Iraq. The government, on the other hand, appoints state or Grand Muftis. Their duties are limited to observing the beginning of lunar months; sending greetings or condolences to the leader and the nation on certain occasions; and issuing technical *fatwa*s on prayer, fasting, pilgrimage, alms, and so forth. And, of course, giving religious legitimacy and support to the ruler as needed.

Scene Seven

Okay, so now we have the *mufti*s, the scholars, the *imam*s in their mosques, the bearded man or covered woman next door—and sometimes they are neither bearded nor covered—each preaching from a different angle and creating a mayhem of confusing opinions and decrees. You think this is too much? Wait until you hear about another major player.

My first time hearing Amr Khaled's name was shortly before the war in 2003. My childhood friend Ammar, who

was living in the U.K., came on a short visit to Baghdad. We
were having dinner at a restaurant overlooking the Tigris
when he mentioned Amr Khaled.

"Amr who?" I asked. Little did I know then that the
name of the Egyptian accountant, born in Alexandria in
1967 would become a trademark of Neo-Islamic evangelism in just a few years.

"You don't know Amr Khaled?" Ammar was shocked
at my ignorance. "He's the best! His weekly show on Iqra
Islamic satellite channel is captivating. All my friends watch
it religiously."

When I googled his name, I got more than five million
results in Arabic, English, and other languages. His official Facebook page alone has over one and a half million
fans, more than three times the number of fans his musical
namesake Amr Diab—a legendary Egyptian pop singer.
An article by Asef Bayat I found in the Egyptian *Al
Ahram Weekly* made an interesting comparison between
the two icons: "Amr Khaled's style resembles that of his
young, affluent audience—cleanly shaven in blue jeans and
polo shirts or in suit and necktie. Khaled simultaneously
embodies the hipness of popular singer Amr Diab." A few
years later, Amr Khaled used the voice of Tamer Hosny,
another flamboyant pop icon, to pep up his show's theme
music for Ramadan.

As I went on browsing his Facebook page, I read that
he'd been chosen by *Newsweek* among its 50 Global Elite
in 2008. He was described as the "anti-bin Laden." Also,
in 2007, he came sixty-second on *Time Magazine*'s list of

the 100 men and women whose power, talent, or moral example is transforming the world. His influence on his viewers was compared to that of Dr. Phil, Pat Robertson, and Rick Warren: "On his TV show and in his frequent public appearances, he told his audiences how much Allah loved people, how merciful Allah was, and how easy it was to earn his forgiveness." Samantha M. Shapiro wrote in an article for the *New York Times*.

It would take forever to read all that has been written about him in the press and media. *The Economist, Huffington Post, The Independent*, BBC News, *The Washington Post*, CBS, *The Sunday Times*, and Reuters... his name is everywhere. Awash in information, I only read bits here and there. This abundance of resources wasn't affordable when Ammar first introduced me in Baghdad to Khaled's realm. All means of communication with the outer world had been strictly censored, often interrupted, and sometimes banned.

Unruly and naturally rebellious, the Iraqis have always gotten their way. Back in the eighties, we watched the BBC's *Top of the Pops* recorded on VHS tapes, secretly brought from London by Iraqi Airways pilots. Just like British teens, we followed the pop chart every week at our homes in Baghdad. Despite risk of fines, confiscation, interrogation, and in several cases, imprisonment, many Iraqis during the nineties defied the laws by installing smuggled satellite dishes on their houses. With curtains closed, they watched dozens of banned channels and recorded their taboo material—porn, political debates, controversial religious sermons—to share with trusted friends and relatives, who'd then pass them on to their own trusted friends and relatives.

Amr Khaled's lectures couldn't possibly have threatened the ruling Ba'athist ruling regime because they were politics-free, revolving around virtues like patience, honesty, humility, compassion, and such. I was excited when I saw a street vendor selling them on DVD and immediately bought a couple to watch with my family. Saddled with high expectations, I must say I was a bit disappointed at the beginning. There was nothing out of the ordinary about the show. I particularly disliked the way Khaled squealed and his eyes jolted open when he got emotional; both seemed so annoyingly weird that I thought of quitting, but for some reason, I didn't. And strangely enough, when the lecture ended after less than an hour, it left everyone in the room, including myself, teary-eyed.

I honestly don't know what it is about Amr Khaled that makes him the phenomenon he is today. I've watched several of his shows since then, but I'm still clueless. Is it his modern clothes or his clean-shaven look? Maybe. And maybe it's the fact that he was the first to step away from the centuries-old Islamic tradition of preaching. Khaled was smart enough to adopt a totally different type of speech to address the audience, playing the role of a consoling friend or a caring neighbor, casting himself as the opposite of the stern, authoritarian, and full-of-clichés sheikhs and *imam*s many Muslims, especially the youth, were fed up with. Also, he relentlessly sifted through ancient books for stories that would have big impact on people. Like a skillful storyteller, he knew exactly how to weave and depict events from the Prophet's life, as well as the other messengers', to move and inspire his Muslim viewers everywhere.

The show's big success consistently put his official website *Amrkhaled.net* among the world's most visited. It appealed more to women and college graduates under the age of twenty-five who browsed from home and school. Amr enjoyed showing off the popularity of his website in his interviews and frequently hinted that it's been competing with Oprah.com. I really wasn't surprised to hear that. In fact, I would go as far as to say that the growing wave of religiosity among educated Arab Muslim youth can largely be attributed to Amr Khaled's lectures. Furthermore, he may also be behind the rocketing sales of headscarves throughout the Arab world. Thousands of girls, including singers and actresses, started wearing *hijab* after listening to his sermons. But his influence didn't stop there.

When Pope Benedict XVI delivered his controversial speech in Regensburg, in 2006, quoting an ancient Byzantine emperor who'd described Islam as violent, evil, and inhuman, tens of thousands of angry Muslims flocked to the streets to protest the Papal assault on their faith. Amr Khaled made the headlines again by calling for calm and issuing an appeal to the Christian churches and leaders titled *A Common Word between Us and You*. "Muslims and Christians together make up well over half of the world's population. Without peace and justice between these two religious communities, there can be no meaningful peace in the world." Inspired by a verse from the Koran and signed by a number of clerics and scholars from different Islamic countries, the letter advanced mutual understanding and mutual respect between the two great religions.

Amr Khaled's ever growing popularity and influence freaked out the authorities in his country. Suspected of having secret ties to the Muslim Brotherhood Society and promoting their doctrine in his popular programs and development projects, Khaled was a constant nuisance to the government, which tried its best to diminish his allure, but all to no avail. After years of pressure and disruptions, he finally gave up and decided to leave Egypt to settle in the U.K., where he would continue to make new shows and pursue his doctorate on peace and coexistence from the University of Wales, Lampeter.

My Egyptian friend Ali told me that Khaled's *Life Makers* program motivated many young men and women to collect clothes and food for the destitute, look after the orphans and the elderly, teach the illiterate and tend the sick. In addition to its Egyptian branches, the Life Makers Society expanded its activities to include other Arab countries as well. Ali, who is a physician, had joined the society and was lecturing to villagers on health and hygiene. He said it made him feel really good about himself.

While I was walking down the street in Amman one day, I caught a glimpse of Amr Khaled's picture printed on a stained piece of paper, randomly stuck on the wall. I stopped to read: *Amr Khaled at Al Hussein Sport City's Arena*. It turned out he was holding a public meeting to promote *Innovators*, his new reality show. *I wouldn't miss that for the world,* I thought. Khaled was and still is very popular in Jordan. Among his audience were Queen Rania and other members of the royal family. The timing of the event, however, seemed rather odd. It had been barely a week since Israel had begun its military offensive against the Gaza Strip, and hundreds of Palestinian casualties were reported. The whole world was outraged, and the Jordanians were living the crisis day by day. They donated blood, food, and other forms of urgent humanitarian aid. In the middle of all this, Amr Khaled was touring the country to announce a new television program!

His yet-to-be-launched reality show was speculated to be an Islamic version of Donald Trump's *The Apprentice,* with groups of young Arab men and women contesting in support of needy families. By that time in 2009, I had lost much of my interest in the genre. Islamic programs were no longer a rare commodity, and Khaled's once-unique model had been copied far and wide. On almost every Arabic channel there was a preacher who dressed like him, talked like him, and even emulated his body language. That said, Amr was far from relying on serendipity. He ventured to explore untapped potentials like reality and self-help shows, and they were paying off incredibly well. But not with me.

As an Iraqi who'd witnessed his homeland being torn apart by religious feuds and conflicts, the last thing I needed was a sermon on how an extra dose of religion could make life bright and beautiful. Still, I was curious to see how his character and presence on stage were going to affect the audience. I took a taxi to the venue an hour before the meeting. A young volunteer, most likely a university student, wearing a shirt that had the new show's logo printed on both sides ushered me inside. Although admission to the event was free, more than half the seats in the arena were vacant because of the ongoing ravaging of Gaza. The organizers insisted the available audience be moved to the sides of the stage in order to give a decent background to Khaled's pictures in the press the next morning.

Aside from my occasional prayers at the mosque, funerals, mourning sessions, and a few weddings, it was my first time attending a sexually segregated spectacle and I must say I wasn't really comfortable with it. I kept reminding myself that it was an Islamic event and we had to abide by the rules. It was good to see some uncovered girls among the female audience on the other side of the stage, nevertheless. After a brief introduction, Khaled walked to the podium, greeted by warm applause from the relatively small attendance. As he started talking, it was obvious that he still had the gestures I disliked the first time I'd seen him video-lecture in Baghdad more than ten years before. It wasn't a big deal now; I had gotten used to them.

Amr spoke passionately about his new show, but it was impossible to ignore the tense situation in Gaza, especially in Jordan, where Palestinians make up a large portion of his fan base. He asked the audience to join in one short prayer for the safety of the helpless civilians, and urged everyone at the venue to make donations to buy new ambulance vehicles for the Gazans under siege. In just a few minutes, a cloud of Khaled's female admirers—covered and uncovered alike—was hovering around him to take pictures. Some of them shook his hands, while others insisted on kissing him on the cheek. He was clearly embarrassed, but probably didn't want to turn them down and appear rude. I thought it was considerate of him to act that way, but the bearded man sitting next to me was totally displeased with the scene. Like him or not, Amr Khaled, in my opinion, will outlive his tenure as a television preacher because he creatively used the material in the *hadith* books to make a difference in the lives of many young Muslims.

Scene Eight

In 2005, a nineteen-year-old girl from the district of Qatif in Saudi Arabia was attacked and gang-raped fourteen times by seven men. On the first of November of the same year, a Saudi court sentenced the attackers to prison terms from ten months to five years although the prosecutor had asked for the death penalty. The raped victim, however, was punished for being in a non-related man's car at the time of the attack. She was first sentenced to ninety lashes, but when she appealed, her punishment was increased to two hundred lashes and six months in prison because of "her attempt to aggravate and influence the judiciary through the media," the Saudi judge explained.

Rape couldn't be proven because the victim had kept silent for a long time. She told no one about her ordeal and had even attempted suicide. On the day she was attacked, the Girl of Qatif, as she's better known today, went to the mall to meet a man who was blackmailing her. He threatened to tell her family about a relationship they'd had on the phone. She was getting married to another man and didn't want anything from the past to disturb her new life. The girl was hoping to retrieve a picture she had sent to her ex-lover.

The verdict aroused international protest and drew harsh criticism for the Saudi judicial system. Then President of the United States George W. Bush expressed anger at a state that did not support the victim, while senators Hillary Clinton and Barack Obama considered the judgment outrageous and beyond unjust. In December 2007, the Saudi monarch finally responded to world outcry and issued a special pardon for the girl.

Less than two years afterward, in February 2009, the district court in Jeddah sentenced another victim of gang-rape—a pregnant twenty-three-year-old—to a year in prison and one hundred lashes. She was found guilty of adultery and of accepting a ride from the stranger who kidnapped her and together with four of his friends raped her all night. The lashes, according to the court, were to be given after the baby's birth. Both verdicts were unspeakably unjust. But these weren't the first times something awful happened in Saudi courts, and I'm afraid it may not be the last.

Saudi Arabia might be the most prominent example of a Sharia-dictated community, but it is definitely not the sole territory. As a matter of fact, Sharia's presence can be detected in civil status and family laws in almost every Islamic country, including the secular ones. Islamist groups in Britain and France have recently voiced demands for the implementation of Sharia in Europe as well. But what does

Sharia mean? The Arabic word *Sharia* itself, which literally translates as *the path*, has acquired negative connotations over the years, implying misogynistic laws and brutal corporal punishments. This widespread conception, while not always accurate, is also not entirely baseless.

Flogging sentences, for example, are commonly issued by Saudi courts for drinking alcohol, whereas stoning is the usual punishment for adultery, and beheading for murder. Such penalties are often carried out in public and have been occasionally covered by the world's media, causing fury and disgust everywhere. Capital punishment is still legal in Iraq and many other Arab and Islamic countries, especially in cases of homicide or rape; but mutilation, lashing, and stoning are all considered illegal. Hanging, according to Iraqi law, is the only method of execution to be used in the country and is not supposed to be conducted in public. However, reality seems to tell a different story. Political opponents in Iraq and many Arab countries have been, and still are, subject to every imaginable form of torture and killing.

That said, there is much more to Sharia than penal codes. Rules of inheritance, marriage, divorce, and parental authority in addition to commercial transactions are all lesser known components of Sharia. Many Sharia rules, such as the weight given to women's testimony as witnesses in court, are regarded by Western lawmakers as degrading, and they actually are. But that wasn't the case when they were introduced in seventh-century Arabia. Not only were the Islamic laws considered revolutionary and progressive in their original environment, they were also regarded as such by the European legislators at that time.

"How many know that until the 18th century, the laws of most European countries authorized torture as an official component of the criminal-justice system? As for sexism, the common law long denied married women any property rights or indeed legal personality apart from their husbands," an article titled "Why Shariah?" by Noah Feldman, a professor at Harvard Law School, published in 2008 in *The New York Times Magazine* read. "When the British applied their law to Muslims in place of Shariah, as they did in some colonies, the result was to strip married women of the property that Islamic law had always granted them—hardly progress towards equality of the sexes," Professor Feldman argued.

Amputation, flogging, and stoning had all been practiced for centuries before the rise of Islam, and they continued to exist for centuries afterwards. The ancient Greeks, Romans, Egyptians, and Babylonians had all implemented them as legal punishments. Lapidation, for example, had been prescribed in Judaism for offences like blasphemy, adultery, or even cursing one's parent. In Deuteronomy 21:18-21, the Bible states that disobedient children should be stoned to death at the gates of their towns. But things have changed since then, and a more humane and constructive approach to dealing with culprits applies in many societies today. The use of physical violence by parents as a means of child-rearing, for example, is outlawed in many European countries.

The way I see Islamic laws is quite similar to the

metaphorical way some Sufis do. Sharia was a candle, providing guidance to people and facilitating their movement at a certain time in history. But candles melt. Our need is for the light, not the candle. In that respect, any other means of illumination like a torch, a fluorescent tube, or maybe a mobile phone light can equally help us walk in the dark without tripping. Sadly, many Muslim jurists, with a few exceptions, place a huge emphasis on the burnt candle. Hence, darkness and crippled movement. And, sometimes, no movement at all.

Scene Nine

Time and again I've given Saudi Arabia as an example. I didn't really have a choice. It's like an archetype for everything that should not be happening, and yet is happening, in Muslim countries. I could also have cited Iran, or Afghanistan under Taliban rule. Both are as regressive and theocratic as Saudi Arabia, possibly more so. I have mentioned them too, but I tend to focus on Saudi Arabia for two basic reasons: first, it's the heartland of Islam, and second, because I know less about life in Iran or Afghanistan than I do about life in Saudi Arabia, an Arab neighbor to my homeland, Iraq.

Saudi sovereigns have always been adamant about retaining the country's Islamic identity, and they've often taken that notion to its extreme. Despite their fancy cars, soaring skyscrapers, and modern conveniences, extremely strict codes of conduct still dictate how the Saudis live their lives. Five times a day, the religious police (or as they prefer to be called, the Committee for the Promotion of Virtue and Prevention of Vice) force all shops to close their doors during prayer time. They beat any adult male caught not praying, and likewise any woman who, according to their personal judgments, is not covering enough. They also beat and arrest all the unmarried couples they find hanging out in the streets.

Whenever I question the humaneness and compatibility of such measures with our time and age, my religious friends would say Saudi Arabia owes its stability and security to its strict application of Sharia. On the surface, this may seem true. Digging a bit deeper, however, reveals quite a different picture.

I have read several books about Omar ibn Al-Khattab, the second caliph in Islam, also known as Al Farouk (the one who is to distinguish between truth and falsehood). Upon his inauguration in Medina in 634, Omar pledged to vigorously chase and punish all transgressors: "He who commits oppression, I shall get on the ground and put my feet right on his cheek until he succumbs to justice. But I will put my cheek to the ground in humility and service for the righteous."

During his ten-year reign as caliph, the Islamic empire expanded far and wide. Muslim armies conquered Syria, Palestine, Egypt, Iraq, and Persia. While state revenues piled up in the central treasury, Omar insisted on living such an ascetic life that he walked the alleys of Medina in a worn, patched garment. It is also said that the caliph—who had once heard the Prophet swear that he'd not hesitate to cut off the hand of his own daughter if she ever committed theft—ordered his son to be flogged in public after he was seen drinking wine. Reportedly, the young man couldn't endure the pain of the whips cutting his naked back and died as he was being lashed.

Although a sincere follower of the Prophet's teachings, Omar wasn't necessarily a literal one. He dared to annul pre-existing rules when there was a need for amendments to be made. In times of severe famine, for example, he suspended cutting off thieves' hands. He also banned temporary marriage, known as *Mut'a* (pleasure), which was common among Muslim warriors during conquests. Caliph Omar ibn Al-Khattab's clear-cut austerity made him much more feared than loved. But popularity was never a priority for him. Since the day he'd become Muslim until his assassination in 644, his life was a constant, tangible manifestation of his faith. Today, Omar is a highly regarded role model for millions of Sunni Muslims, including the Saudi royals. Or so they claim.

Scene Ten

The fear of extreme punishment has indeed made Saudi Arabia a safe land. Although crime rates there have risen, they are still low compared with other countries. Inevitable questions: Is Saudi Arabia a perfect utopian model? Is it the modern equivalent of the Islamic state under the Prophet or Caliph Omar? I'm afraid not.

It's no secret that Saudi princes and princesses today enjoy a lavish lifestyle where every single desire, no matter how vain or sinful, has to be met. Their stories have long been making headlines in the Western press with accusations of drug-trafficking, illegal arms trade, money-laundering, sexual abuse, rape, and even murder. Prince Al-Waleed bin Talal, nephew of the Saudi king, ranked twenty-ninth on the *Forbes* list of the world's billionaires in 2012. With large stakes in Citigroup, AOL, Four Seasons Hotels, Euro Disney, Apple, and Fairmont Hotels, and with a fortune estimated at twenty-six billion dollars, it wasn't his first time on the list. Since 1997, the prince has been a regular on the list, and he even made the top five in 2003. *His palaces and real estate are worth more than $3 billion. Owns jewelry collection he values at $730 million, plus 4 airplanes, including an Airbus A380,* Forbes wrote in 2010.

It's unquestionably a very rich country. Saudi Arabia has been the world's top oil producer for quite a long time now. But despite its massive revenues, beggars and slums are not uncommon in Saudi cities. Ilan Berman, a specialist in Middle Eastern affairs, wrote an interesting article in Forbes in 2010, "Saudi Arabia's House of Cards." Berman, along with other observers and commentators, blames much of the poverty in the country on the royal family. "Average Saudis have experienced a devastating reversal of economic fortune, even as the royal cohort that rules over them has become more numerous, indulgent, and bloated."

Strict Sharia codes and punishments have obviously failed to accomplish goals in Saudi Arabia. In fact, they have empowered the rulers to further persecute people and have resulted in mass corruption and tyranny. But Saudi royals are not the only ones who don't abide by the rules. Although the punishment for drinking is public lashing, smuggled alcoholic beverages can still be found in many Saudi homes. And for the Saudis who don't enjoy drinking in secret, all they need to do is drive to neighboring Bahrain, where they can drink all they want on weekends. Thailand and Lebanon are favorite destinations for many Saudi men, as well: they can fulfill their every sexual fantasy without any fear of punishment. When I visited Bangkok many years ago, Thai pimps confused me for a Saudi and stopped me on the street to show me their catalogues of whores. Much to their chagrin, I was just a low-budget Iraqi tourist.

Scene Eleven

The most confusing thing about Sharia in my opinion is that there is no single reference, no *Book of Sharia* to which all Muslims can turn for guidance. Interpretations and opinions, again, are all we have. While both countries force women to cover their hair in the name of Sharia, Iranian women are allowed to drive cars, but Saudi women are totally banned from driving. This means there are two different versions of Sharia: Iranian and Saudi, Shia and Sunni. Well, not exactly, because there is practically no limit to the number of existing versions of Sharia in the Islamic world.

In 2002, the Saudi Committee for the Promotion of Virtue and Prevention of Vice caused the death of fifteen innocent girls whose school in Mecca was on fire. They prevented the terrified teenagers from leaving the building and hindered passersby and rescue workers from entering the school to put out the fire because the girls had forgotten to put on their additional black cloaks and headscarves while panicking and stampeding to flee the blaze. The religious policemen decided—based on their own ad-libbed version of Sharia—that they should lock the girls inside lest they be seen uncovered by the strangers on the street. They left them to die behind the gate.

Scene Twelve

President Barack Obama quoted the Prophet in his speech at the National Prayer Breakfast on February 5, 2009: "In Islam, there is the *hadith* that reads, *None of you truly believes until he wishes for his brother what he wishes for himself.*" It is almost impossible to have a conversation about Islam without coming across one or more of Mohammed's sayings. But while some *hadiths* are very specific, others are rather figurative, and are therefore prone to all types of interpretations—and, sometimes, exploitation. Any Muslim today can find a *hadith* to justify whatever he or she wants to do, good or bad.

Just recently, I saw an interview on television with a Bedouin man who had more than eighty sons and was determined to father a hundred. To achieve his goal, he married an eighteen-year-old girl, almost fifty years his junior. But since Muslim men can only have four wives at a time, he had to divorce the wives who, because of age, had become infertile. The old man seemed very proud of his sexual potency. He claimed to have been having intercourse seven times each day, and he giggled happily at his nickname

Casanova. When the interviewer asked him about the real incentive behind making his colony of wives and sons, he answered that it was all religious. He was simply following the Prophet's teachings.

This Bedouin Casanova didn't say that he'd been collecting wives and mass-producing children because he was feeling some sort of emotional insecurity deep down inside, nor did he admit that he only wanted to satisfy his insatiable sex drive at any cost. That would have sounded shamefully mundane—although he did hint at the sex thing. Instead, he hid his insecurity and lust behind a veil of religious devoutness that would make them more dignified and even honorable. His claim wasn't totally baseless, either. There is indeed a *hadith* that urges Muslims to beget as many children as they can, for the Prophet will take pride in our number on Judgment Day. The *hadith* doesn't suggest how the parents are supposed to protect and feed their clans, though, let alone educate them.

Different Hadiths

Qudsi, or Sacred *Hadiths*, are sayings of the Prophet, in which there are neither rules nor warnings, but rather a description of the Divine and His infinite mercy, love, and forgiveness. When I first read them, it occurred to me that not a single person on the face of the Earth, no matter how errant or sinful, with just a little faith in their hearts, will ever be left to burn in hell. God is compassionate and will eventually forgive everyone. "My mercy prevails over my wrath," He said through His messenger Mohammed in one of the *Qudsi Hadiths*. I found the sayings so comforting that I kept going back to them each time I encountered problems in my life. They became my spiritual sanctuary. But beautiful as they are, the *Qudsi Hadiths* are much less quoted by Muslim scholars and clerics compared to the other—more jurisprudential, less spiritual—sayings of the Prophet. Why? I have no idea.

My Hadith

Like a fisherman battling a stormy ocean, I threw out my net into the books of *hadith*. One night, as I drew it in, there came a precious catch that would change forever the way I approached religion. It took me to the source of my being and enabled me to access innate wisdom I never knew I had. The words were so heartfelt that I never needed to question their authenticity like I usually do with the other sayings.

According to the story, a man walked right up to Mohammed and asked him about virtue and sin. The Prophet put his hand on the man's chest and told him thrice, "Consult your heart. Consult your soul." He then added, "Virtue is that which comforts your heart and calms your soul. And sin is that which disturbs your soul and troubles your chest even if people judge otherwise."

When I read that *hadith*, I realized how foolish it had been to blame myself for making choices that felt right, yet somehow didn't conform to mainstream Islam. Without knowing it, I was practicing what the Prophet had told the Arabian man to do: I was listening to my heart, and my heart told me that it wasn't right to scorn people just because they were different. It told me that there was no one path to God, so there was therefore no reason for me to consider the people who walked a different pathway than mine as my enemies. My heart told me that women are by no means inferior to men, or laymen to clergymen, or non-Muslims to Muslims. It was an awareness badly needed while treading on the bridge. Now that I know I have the compass inside me, all I have to do is go in the direction the needle is pointing. And I always will.

Works Cited

Chapter 2

- Definition of *balance*, noun 5b. Merriam-Webster. (http://www.merriam-webster.com/dictionary/balance)

Chapter 3

- Zeidan, Youssef. *Al-Nabati*. Cairo: Dar El Shorouk, 2010

Chapter 5

- *A Single Man*. Dir. Tom Ford. Perf. Colin Firth and Julianne Moore. The Weinstein Company, 2009

Chapter 7

- "Theory and implementation". Sheikh Zayed Grand Mosque Center. (http://www.szgmc.ae/en/theory-and-implementation)
- "Message of the Mosque". Sheikh Zayed Grand Mosque Center. (http://www.szgmc.ae/en/message-of-the-mosque)

Chapter 8

- "New Independence for Al-Azhar". Egypt Chapter, 2013 Annual Report, United States Commission on International Religious Freedom.
- Liston, Broward. "Interview: Missionary Work in Iraq." *Time*, April 15, 2003

Chapter 10

- *Mohammad, Messenger of God/ The Message.* Dir. Moustapha Akkad. Perf. Anthony Quinn and Irene Papas. Screenplay: H.A.L. Craig. Tarik Films Distributors, 1976
- Steyn, Mark. "Moustapha, Messenger of Hollywood." *Atlantic*, JAN/ FEB 2006
- Zoakos, Criton. "Anglo-Soviet condominium in Mideast supplants U.S.A." *EIR International.* Volume11, Number15, April17, 1984

Chapter 13

- Houtsma, Martin Theodor. *E. J. Brill's First Encyclopedia of Islam, 1913- 1936.* Imprint: Leiden, E. J. Brill, 1987
- Bayat, Asef. "From Amr Diab to Amr Khaled: Faith and fun; can one have it all?" *Al-Ahram Weekly.* Issue No. 639, 22 - 28 May 2003
- "The Newsweek 50, 48: Amr Khaled, Egyptian televangelist." *Newsweek*, December 19, 2008

- Nomani, Asra. "The Time 100, Heroes & Pioneers: Amr Khaled." *Time*, May, 03, 2007
- Shapiro, Samantha M. "Ministering to the Upwardly Mobile Muslim." *The New York Times, Magazine*. April 30, 2006
- Audience Snapshot, amrkhaled.net. Alexa. (http://www.alexa.com/siteinfo/amrkhaled.net)
- "The ACW Letter (Summary and Abridgement)." A Common Word, October, 13, 2007
- "Saudi Rape Victim Gets 200 Lashes." CBS/Associated Press, February 11, 2009
- Feldman, Noah. "Why Shariah?" *The New York Times, Magazine*. March 16, 2008
- Cordesman, Anthony H. "Saudi Arabia's Internal Security Forces: The Commission for the Promotion of Virtue and Prevention of Vice or Religious Police." *Saudi Arabia: National Security in a Troubled Region*. ABC-CLIO, 2009
- "The World's Billionaires, #19 Prince Alwaleed Bin Talal Alsaud." Forbes.com. (http://www.forbes.com/lists/2010/10/billionaires-2010_Prince-Alwaleed-Bin-Talal-Alsaud_0RD0.html)
- Berman, Ilan. "Saudi Arabia's House of Cards" *Forbes*, July 13, 2010
- "Saudi police 'stopped' fire rescue." BBC News, March 15, 2002

Author's Note

Rejection, unlike what many would imagine, is not always a writer's worst nightmare. Well, at least it's not mine! Although undeniably a very unpleasant experience, I'd rather be rejected than accepted and have my manuscript transformed into a different book under pressures from the literary agent, editor, or publisher. Or maybe all three of them. I had read several complaints about that, and it was my biggest fear when I decided that it was time to stop what seemed like an endless circle of polishing and re-polishing, and have an expert's opinion about my book. Of course, I was well aware that the script needed a lot of work before being ready for publication. I was okay with making some changes here and there, but I wasn't, for instance, willing to compromise the book's backbone; its structure, which, thankfully, I didn't have to.

By sheer coincidence I stumbled upon Signal 8 Press while web-browsing. No sooner did I exchange a few emails with Marshall Moore—an American author who'd undergone many hardships with publishers before launching his own publishing company in Hong Kong—than I was convinced I had found what I had been looking for. I knew that he'd go through my scenes with both respect and professionalism, and I couldn't ask for more.

I'd long pledged myself not to write an acknowledgment.

I thought acknowledgments were often pretentious and full of clichés. Now that we are done with editing, or almost; I find myself obliged to reconsider my pledge. I must thank Signal 8 Press and Marshall Moore for having faith in my project, and most importantly, for not distorting my work of almost five years, but rather helping me enhance its original merit. Thank you very much indeed.